THE RECIPE FOR
SUCCESS
IN
Optimizing
YOUR GUEST
EXPERIENCE

THE RECIPE FOR

SUCCESS

IN

Optimizing

YOUR GUEST

EXPERIENCE

DERYK D. DAVIDSON

THE RECIPE FOR SUCCESS IN OPTIMIZING YOUR GUEST EXPERIENCE

REQUIRED READING FOR THE MODERN-DAY RESTAURANT

BY DERYK D. DAVIDSON

Published by:
The Hospitality Edge, Inc.
HospitalityEdge.net

Book Design and Publishing Support by
PearCreative.ca

Photography by Deryk Davidson
Author photo by Coline Martinez

ISBN: 979-8-9943329-0-0 (paperback)
ISBN: 979-8-9943329-1-7 (hardcover)
ISBN: 979-8-9943329-3-1 (hardcover full color)
ISBN: 979-8-9943329-2-4 (ebook)

"I cannot teach anybody anything.
I can only make them think."

Socrates

CONTENTS

PREFACE

For as long as I can remember, I have found myself observing restaurant staff as they perform their duties. From the initial greeter and server to the general manager and bartender—if they are working, I am observing! And the type of establishment is irrelevant. From visiting the lowliest dive bars in the Deep Ellum neighborhood of Dallas, Texas, to Sonoma, California's the girl & the fig or Georges Perrier's Philadelphia five-star-awarded French restaurant Le Bec-Fin (may it rest in peace), I was always watching, and I have seen it all!

Also, let us be honest, besides the quality of the food, the staff is the most critical area of a restaurant and one that requires the most attention. Poorly performing team members can hold back or even sink an eatery. For me, it is impossible *not to watch* the staff's behavior and to see what they get right or where they have simply missed the boat completely. Therefore, this book combines my experience and observations to produce my *recipes for success,* and points to ponder, for those restaurateurs and managers in the biz.

I was born in Sunrise, Florida, and moved to Boulder, Colorado, to begin junior high school in the seventh grade. As I grew up and moved into my adulthood, I took the restaurant or hospitality route, rather than the "retail" one—that is, I worked in the restaurant business, or "biz," rather than retail stores such as clothing or grocery. My first job was as a busser at the Lotus Pavilion, a Chinese restaurant on the downtown Pearl Street Mall in Boulder. That was an interesting ride for a young man, but one that got me hooked on the restaurant business.

Aside from that first job, most subsequent ones were also in the biz, until I finished graduate school. In graduate school, I received a Master of Arts in Industrial & Organizational Psychology, which could be broadly defined as applying research to improve the well-being and performance of people and their organizations, including job motivation, implementing teams and facilitating organizational change. This M.A. degree coupled with real-world experience has created a focused mindset when encountering the human component in a business environment. The objective when compiling my thoughts for this book, and what to include, centered around the idea of a straightforward read for anyone in the biz, from the newly opened to the well-established restaurant owner or manager. Furthermore, I realized that the type of restaurant is immaterial, though I believe that fine dining and sit-down styles will benefit the most. This book covers many areas of an eatery but is primarily focused on two general areas: unique selling points or propositions (USP), and the user, or guest, dining experience (UX).

- **USP:** A restaurant's focus on how to achieve a product- or service-based unique selling point or proposition (USP) with the goal of differentiating itself from other eating establishments. This could include a unique location or inside built-out feature, food items, drink items, decor...

- **UX:** Providing the best experience for the guest when they enter the business's environment and interact with its team members.

Both areas permeate the book and are explored in greater detail. Please…read on.

ACKNOWLEDGMENTS

Thanks to the staff at my local south Florida Starbucks for providing friendly service and an endless flow of coffee.

Thank you Patrick O'Keefe and Shannon Van Woerden of Kaluz Restaurant Group and Billy's Stone Crab ownership and management for your time and for allowing me to photograph your beautiful restaurant.

Thank you to the hospitality management staff at the Harbor Beach Marriott Resort & Spa and Kaitlin Harris of The Zimmerman Agency for being extremely helpful and flexible with the shoot schedule.

Thank you Elena, Garvin, Lindsay, Stephen and Tobias for taking the time out of your busy days to work through my questions and to make your invaluable contributions to this book!

Thank you Coline Martinez, Dayre Davidson, Laura Satterly, Liza Rubin Mendelson and Rory Rolfs for your support and for lending a helpful ear.

Thank you Jennifer Guarino for your eternal patience with my draft review requests and acting as a general sound board when I found myself searching for just the right word.

CONTRIBUTORS

These contributors' inputs appear throughout the book and are identified by a line along the left margin for easy recognition.

TOBIAS FROEHLICH
GENERAL MANAGER

Tobias Froehlich's career has been defined by leadership, growth and a relentless pursuit of excellence. Beginning as General Manager of Via Vite in Cincinnati, he quickly established himself as a strong operator with a gift for building teams and elevating guest experiences. His path led him to Washington, D.C., where he joined Hive Hospitality and rose through the ranks at its Michelin-starred restaurants, Bresca and Jônt. There, Tobias sharpened his ability to lead at the highest level of dining, overseeing operations that demanded both precision and creativity. Today, as General Manager of MAASS, Tobias continues to set the tone for excellence—driving culture, inspiring teams and ensuring every guest experience is nothing short of exceptional.

MAASS, Fort Lauderdale, FL (Hive Hospitality)

- General Manager | 2024–Present
- Currently overseeing operations at MAASS, a Michelin-starred concept within the Four Seasons Hotel, where the Chef's Counter offers an immersive fine dining experience

Bresca Washington, D.C. (Hive Hospitality)
Jônt Washington, D.C. (Hive Hospitality)

- Jônt is a 17-seat chef's counter located above Bresca
- Management Support | November 2023–Present
- Led operations for Bresca, a Michelin one-star restaurant, and Jônt, a Michelin two-star restaurant

Ritz-Carlton West End, Washington, D.C.—Saga and Quadrant

- General Manager
- Managed service and operations at Saga and Quadrant, elevating luxury dining within a Forbes Five-Star property

Sfoglina, Fabio Trabocchi Restaurant Group, Washington, D.C.

- General Manager
- Led front-of-house operations for one of the city's premier Italian restaurants, part of the acclaimed Fabio Trabocchi Restaurant Group

Via Vite, Cincinnati, OH

- General Manager

Oversaw operations at one of Cincinnati's landmark Italian restaurants on Fountain Square.

ELENA HERSHEY
FORMER OWNER-OPERATOR, BILLY'S STONE CRAB, INC.

Elena Hershey, known as Mrs. Billy, was the driving force behind Billy's Stone Crab. For more than two decades, Elena worked side by side with Billy—supporting the team, managing finances, expanding their presence, elevating the brand and cultivating the restaurant's spirit both in person and across social media platforms. As the wife of the late Billy Hershey, she helped turn their beloved dockside seafood restaurant into a world-known seafood destination. Elena brought heart, vision and elegance to the business, shaping its legacy of excellence. After Billy's passing, Elena stepped into a new chapter with her brand, Elena Hershey/Mrs. Billy's, carrying forward the values that made Billy's iconic. She continues to lead with passion through real estate, philanthropy and beyond.

Billy's Stone Crab Restaurant and Fisheries, Hollywood Beach Florida
- Owner-operator | 1998–2019

LINDSAY LIPOVICH-MOTT
MANAGING OWNER-OPERATOR, WINNIFRED INC.

Lindsay Lipovich has spent more than two decades in the bar and restaurant industry, beginning her journey as a busser at a country club before earning her degree in Visual Communication from Penn State. In 2014, she opened her first restaurant and soon after launched Lilo's Streetfood and Bar in Lake Worth Beach, Florida, which has been a local favorite since 2016. Known for her eye for partnerships and talent for bringing great people together, Lindsay continues to grow her business with creativity, vision and community at the heart of it all. Lindsay has thought outside the box her entire career. At Lilo's, she transformed unused space into The Library, a hidden speakeasy specializing in craft cocktails served in an intimate setting. During the challenges of the COVID-19 pandemic, she introduced BRK Republic, South Florida's first dog bar, bringing a one-of-a-kind concept to the community. In 2023, she revived a 40-year-old restaurant space with the creation of Lantern Local Tavern, blending tradition with a fresh, modern energy. She is always thinking about what's next!

Lilo's Streetfood and Bar, Lake Worth Beach, Florida, since 2016

Library Speakeasy, Lake Worth Beach, Florida, since 2018

BRK Republic, West Palm Beach, Florida, since 2020

Lantern Local Tavern, Lantana, Florida, since 2023

Lucky's Bar, West Palm Beach, Florida, since 2024

GARVIN MOISE
CERTIFIED GENERAL MANAGER

First Watch Restaurants, Inc., Plantation, Florida
- Founded in 1983, currently with 580 locations across 31 states
- Certified General Manager | Sept 2025–Present

Rising through the ranks since 2019

STEPHEN SIDLO
VICE PRESIDENT OPERATIONS

Stephen is a dynamic and visionary leader in the hospitality industry, recognized for his collaborative approach and ability to inspire high-performing teams. With a strong focus on team building, he creates environments where individuals feel valued, motivated and empowered to excel. Stephen is an outside-the-box thinker who embraces innovation to solve complex challenges and drive measurable results. His leadership style is defined by patience, wisdom and a calm presence, allowing him to guide teams through change while maintaining clarity and focus. With a sharp ability to see the bigger picture, Stephen balances strategic thinking with hands-on execution. He is committed to fostering a culture of trust, accountability and continuous improvement, making him a respected and influential force in the industry. In 2025, Stephen received from the Marquis Who's Who Publications Board the "Who's Who in America" award.

Anthony's Coal Fired Pizza

- Founded in 2002, currently with 50 locations across six states.
- Vice President Operations | March 2025–Present
- Manages 26 locations throughout Florida

Doc B's Restaurant & Bar, Fort Lauderdale, Florida

- Founded in Chicago in 2013, currently with ten locations across four states.
- Regional Manager

True Food Kitchen, Atlanta, Georgia

- Founded in Phoenix, Arizona, in 2008, currently with 46 locations across 18 states.
- Senior Manager

INTRODUCTION

Why should you read this book?

The National Restaurant Association recognizes a first-year 30% failure rate in the restaurant industry. This book aims to help you improve your USP and UX to maximize your chances of avoiding becoming a part of this stat.

And if you make it past the first year, it's a large and competitive market. In Florida, for example, 2022 statistics from the National Restaurant Association and Bureau of Labor Statistics show that 47,052 eating and drinking locations took in a total of $69.4 billion in estimated sales. If you're reading this in Florida: How much of that did you capture? Or, conversely, how much of that did you lose— "opportunity lost," if you will?

Do you remember why you opened a restaurant? Was it simply to survive, or to be your own boss? I am thinking not. I am guessing it was to thrive and operate a successful, profitable eatery that you would be proud of and that the public would adore. So where did you land? Ask yourself, do you want to be considered yesterday's news or tomorrow's place to be?

Within these pages I share my observations from my experiences working in everything from corporate-owned chains or high-star-rated restaurants to a beloved iconic converted house eatery. In addition, as my work and leisure travels have taken me to 42 states, I have also included lessons from the steak houses, quirky coffee shops and fine dining eateries that I've visited. After you've read this book and extracted from it those parts you find applicable right now, you can use it as a reference guide to review your business periodically.

In addition to my master's degree, I am also a senior project manager and have worked for organizations across various industries. I have consulted with technology companies and trained Fortune 150 company employees on the SAP application. I possess multiple credentials, including the PMP and Lean Six Sigma Green Belt, and have successfully completed countless projects with approved multi-million-dollar budgets. Systems, processes, best practices and standards are prevalent in my life and are germane to the topics in this book. Without organization and self-discipline, some goals may take longer to realize, if they can be achieved at all.

This book goes beyond my recommendations based on my experience. However, I have also included suggestions and best practices from successful restaurateurs, seasoned restaurant employees and successful businesspersons. Their input throughout this book offers further ideas and comparisons, because there can be multiple ways to accomplish something. Incorporating these points of view, successes and failures reveals a world where no one can predict the future with absolute certainty. There is no guarantee that a business or concept will succeed. These contributions provide a broader perspective from which we all can learn.

Your goal in reading this book is to have an open mind, learn from these tales of past experiences and then apply the best practices presented here to place yourself into a better position to succeed. One based on knowledge and others' lessons learned.

Part I focuses on identifying your unique selling point or proposition and planning for the customer experience you want to offer. It includes case studies from other industries as well as tips on advertising and marketing.

Part II goes into more detail on how each part of the business contributes to user experience, from the staff members who clean restrooms or wash dishes to the managers and greeters. *Every* employee affects your UX and therefore your success. Accordingly, this part devotes a chapter to each area, highlighting the key day-to-day responsibilities and actions that affect UX, as well as the longer-term, behind-the-scenes considerations that can keep your business moving forward.

Along the way, you may be exposed to a new term or see an expression used in a way you were not familiar with. This book is not about giving you an exhaustive list of terms or idioms but instead explains some commonly used ones that come up as we discuss each topic. There's a list of the terms and their explanations in a glossary in Part III. The intent is to help you to understand the basic concepts, responsibilities, roles and tangible items, and how these work together to form a "whole" of the restaurant and the experience that the guest, *your guest*, will receive. This book is not a comprehensive *How To Open* or *How To Run a Restaurant from A to Z*. Instead, we keep our primary focus on the USP and UX.

In today's environment, a successful restaurant needs to get it right, *all of it right*. *Why* must they get it *all* right? Because the guest that walks into a restaurant today could be from any age group—Baby Boomers, Generation X, Millennials or Generation Z—and each of these generations has vastly different preferences and motivators when considering where to dine. Therefore, as you do not know *who* will patronize your eatery and what drives them, you must be prepared for *any* guest from *any* generation. We will circle back to this in chapter 2.

> "The whole is greater than the sum of its parts."
>
> —an often-referenced quote
> attributed to Greek philosopher Aristotle

> "Don't sweat the small stuff."
> "Focus on the big picture."
> "See the forest but be mindful of the trees."

Do not get mired down in the nitty-gritty when you need to be viewing something from the 50,000-foot level. Conversely, do not take a bird's-eye view when you should be up close and personal. Use common sense. Stop. Think. And very importantly, keep in mind what works best for *your* restaurant.

STOP AND REFLECT

When you see this "stop symbol," it means you should Stop and Reflect, to dive deeper on what you have just read—for example:

- What does it mean to you?

- How would you define it?
- Can you envision it?
- Does it add value?
- Is that acceptable to you?
- What are you trying to accomplish or avoid?

This book provides guidelines, instruction, food for thought, while possibly requiring a mindset shift to realize the best returns. The "hard costs" involved may be minimal, while sweat equity, perseverance, patience and steadfastness will make up the bulk of the effort involved. There is no magic bullet. And there is no one answer or solution that fits every situation.

By instilling in yourself and your staff what you capture *and embrace* from these chapters, your house can accomplish remarkable things.

PART I

IDENTIFYING USP AND DESIGNING UX

Chapter 1

LESSONS FROM
OTHER INDUSTRIES

The hospitality industry, and specifically restaurants, is unique among businesses with its immediately consumed product offerings, notable use of gratuities and high staff turnover rates. But at the end of the day restaurants are *still* a business. So why does it appear many owners do not treat them as such but instead as something much more casual? Many operating procedures and best practices that are standard in other businesses can and should also be applied to a restaurant. And the best practices surrounding the human element are as critical as the quality of the meals being served. The information below does not come from famous restaurant owners or television celebrities. Nary a Gordon Ramsey or Anthony Bourdain among them. But their words are just as powerful and germane.

STOP AND REFLECT

Question: Do you hire a server, bartender or cook, onboard them, set their schedule and then let 'em loose without any oversight or future evaluation? Imagine an accounting or law firm hiring a Certified Public Accountant or attorney and *not* having an evaluation schedule. How about a store manager for a big-box operation?

Is your business any different than any other when it comes to ensuring the employees (staff) possess the requisite skills and remain in alignment with the company's strategic short—and long-term plans?

Farzad and Rhonda Dibachi[1] talk about creating productive workplaces and motivating employees and propose a two-step process to produce "transparency" and "accountability management." To summarize, my interpretation of this process is that "transparency" means all members of a company understand what their role in the greater scheme is, they understand how their work influences the success of the company, which enables them to make good decisions based on senior leadership's priorities and use the company's assets to assist in reaching these corporate goals. This is accomplished when managers maintain a professional culture that is focused on results. And by the

---

1   *Just Add Management: Seven Steps to Creating a Productive Workplace and Motivating Your Employees In Challenging Times*, Farzad and Rhonda Dibachi, McGraw Hill, 2003.

way, maintaining this culture does not mean you can't also have a fun workplace. In "accountability management," managers need to identify and communicate the business's priorities. Whereas in my project management world, we may use *information radiators* (a visual display of information in very visible locations such as hallways so team members can see the latest data being broadcast), "accountability management" is the enforcement of processes. It involves tracking the employees' progress and making them accountable.

Does anyone in *your* business, who knows the restaurant's goals and objectives, verify regularly that the staff is in alignment with those goals and objectives? The so-called "hard" skills—those they need to do the basic job—are apparent, because if they didn't have those skills, you would give them training or, if they still couldn't perform, would most likely terminate their employment. But these hard skills *still* need to be kept in focus and reviewed on a consistent basis. Otherwise, the meal presentation, amount of alcohol in a drink, seating procedures in busy times, etc. may be out of sync with management's directives. And what about the "soft" skills? How much emphasis is placed on those, and who keeps a watchful eye on staff to ensure the entire team is in alignment? The front of house (FOH) manager? Back of house (BOH) manager? Team leads? General manager (GM)? The correct answer is... all the above.

> "Soft skills enhance customer service: Jobs that involve interacting with customers, clients or patients require strong soft skills like communication, problem-solving, and empathy. While hard skills may be important for providing specific services, it's the soft skills that enable employees to provide excellent customer service."
>
> **GREG GOLDSHTEYN**
> Manager, Quality Assurance, Executive MBA

Are your greeters appropriately dressed, smiling and engaging when talking with the guests? Once guests are seated, are they approached within the agreed-upon time? Would the appearance of the main dish achieve approval from the executive chef, GM and BOH manager? And if not, would the server, your first line of defense, know how to react and what to do?

STOP AND REFLECT

Can you see that if any one of these were not up to the restaurant's standards (assuming standards exist), it would be considered a miss? Do you recognize this and how it could be received negatively? Now imagine if two or three things were not up to par...you have just provided a negative UX, a potential negative written review or opinion spread through word of mouth or, worse, on social media.

INSPIRATION FROM ANOTHER SECTOR: ELECTRONIC HEALTH RECORDS (EHR)

You know those patients' records of your hospital and doctor's visits? Let's talk about Epic Systems, a privately held healthcare software company in the United States, and what makes them special.

"Epic develops software to help people get well, help people stay well, and help future generations be healthier."[2]

- *The company has a 36% market share of U.S. hospitals' (electronic health records) software.*[3]
- Judith R. Faulkner, 43% shareholder, CEO and founder of Epic Systems, has a framed affirmation hanging at Epic: *"Don't be a champion of the mediocre."*
- Epic pours *38% of its operating expense into research and development,* or the type of investments that can deliver game-changing innovation.
- *The company has a 60% market share* among health systems and academic medical centers. Epic now will be used by every health system on U.S. News & World Report's best hospitals list, with *>90% of the country's medical students* being trained on Epic systems.[4]

Epic Systems produces all its software; has never grown by acquisition; and healthcare systems choose Epic more than *anyone else in the market.* Their systems provide real and noticeable advantages in terms of continuity of quality care, sharing information and improving communication between a healthcare provider and a patient—integration across

---

2   epic.com/about
3   Forbes: February 26, 2024.
4   Forbes.com, February 26, 2024.

products, interoperability with critical partners, ability to standardize healthcare workflows, and constant technological development.

Let's talk a little bit about USP. Remember, a USP, or unique selling point, differentiates a company from its competitors. Usually, this is around better or perceived better product offerings, price, quality, service, uniqueness or a combination thereof. In Epic's case, it is a combination of controlling quality by keeping all development in-house. By adhering to strict processes and proven implementation methods when installing and integrating with other applications. By funneling 38% of its operating expense into research and development to continuously improve compatibility with other software applications to ensure seamless communication of data. The team at Epic believe in themselves. They pour real dollars into ensuring their competitive advantage...not just for today but for tomorrow.

> >90% of the country's medical students are trained in Epic systems. Why do you think that is?

Companies choose Epic because they can count on them being there and consistently offering a quality product...being compatible with their legacy systems...continuously improving their product offerings...removing some pain from installing a new EHR system across an entire healthcare system. That's why they choose Epic.

STOP AND REFLECT

Why does a customer choose your restaurant?

- Is it the quality of your food?
- The quality of your service?
- The consistency of your food?
- The comfortable, clean and fresh environment (e.g., no worn-out plates, flatware, glasses, furniture, menus; maintained painted walls, modern decor)?
- Conversely, why may a customer not choose your restaurant?

INSPIRATION FROM ANOTHER SECTOR: SHARKS AND BASKETBALL

ABC reality television series *Shark Tank* member and owner of Dallas Mavericks, Mark Cuban says he was "a lousy employee"—and that was key to his success.[5] "I was never going to be good at working for someone else," he stated. So, he began honing his sales skills.

When you're great at sales, as Cuban says he is, "you understand what people need and want, [and] you put yourself in a position to help them," he said in a TikTok interview.

---

5   CNBC *Make It*, November 24, 2023.

In that sense, salesmanship is the sort of practical skill that can help you become successful in nearly any field, once you have mastered it, according to Cuban.

Mark's first tech startup was in 1989. His sales pitch relied on his No. 1 key for making a sale, which he learned at age 12 while selling garbage bags door-to-door: "You're not trying to convince people. You're trying to help them," as Cuban told *GQ* magazine. "It's all about putting myself in your shoes," he added. "It's, 'I really think that this can be a better solution for you. And if I find you a better solution, will you do business with me?'"

STOP AND REFLECT

In your restaurant:

- Do you understand what your customer needs and wants?
- Do you put yourself in a position to understand?
- Do your staff listen to their guests, and elicit feedback?
- Do your staff put themselves in their guests' shoes to see what they see and experience?
  - And if so, how do you know?

I hope you have paused and reflected on these companies and people, and their calls to action (CTAs). You can see from these *non-restaurateurs* what they stand for and how they conduct business while clearly backing it up with amazing results. Their mindset is as applicable to you in your hospitality world as it is to them in their non-eatery ones. Now, it is time to get busy. Are you ready?

Chapter 2

LET'S IDENTIFY GOALS AND MAKE SURE EVERYONE KNOWS THEM

Where do we go from here? We, or more precisely, *you*, need to jump in now—it is time to start taking the necessary steps to identify your restaurant's goals. Time to start the discussions, gather requirements and set timetables. This is not just to ensure that all moving parts of your business are working in harmony, but also to confirm what needs to be achieved and that all relevant parties are on board. This understanding is needed *before* proceeding, because these details will shape your plans.

Your strategy and your potential for success are the culmination of *many things*. Use your best judgement.

If your restaurant does not use all the role titles I reference, e.g., GM, FOH Manager or BOH Manager with their stated duties, simply replace them with your equivalents.

 According to some experts, anticipation of a stressor can be at least as stressful as its actual occurrence and often more so.[6] Take skydiving, for instance. Much of the stress will be experienced *before* the actual act of falling out of an airplane with just the thought of the jump producing stress and physical manifestations. But once you take the leap, so to speak, the stress is immediately reduced, if not gone completely. Procrastination is to "put off intentionally and habitually; put off intentionally the doing of something that should be done." Is it fear of the unknown, decision paralysis? Don't give in to it! Start taking the necessary steps for your jump!

> "Be willing to make decisions. That's the most important quality in a good leader. Don't fall victim to what I call the Ready, Aim-Aim-Aim Syndrome. You must be willing to fire."
>
> **T. BOONE PICKENS**
> American business magnate and financier

---

6   *Health Psychology*, 2nd Ed. Shelley E. Taylor, 1991.

STOP AND REFLECT

Let us get started with a few questions. For example:

- If you own a restaurant, why?
- What characteristics do you champion in the business?
- What are your specific goals or aspirations as a manager or owner?
- Outperform your competition?
- Stand out from your competition?
- Fill a void in the marketplace?

Do any of the following align with your responses? Would they align from your *guests'* perspective?

- The quality of the food and its preparation accuracy
- The quality of the service
- The restaurant's temperature or ambiance
- The cleanliness of the dining areas
- The perceived value of the menu items

To avoid derailment, the restaurant's *strategic goals* should be known, well defined *and* embraced by management and staff. For lasting change, you need to know what you want to accomplish, why you chose those goals, how you plan on succeeding, what will be the measure of success and how you plan on tracking progress. If feedback or research has provided insight into what the guest is seeking, one way to facilitate this process is to frame your goals from the user's or guest's perspective. For example:

"As a (guest), I want (to be approached within two minutes of sitting) so that (I can order a drink before my meal)."

These "user stories" should be written down and could provide the jumping-off point for additional discussions with management and staff to further refine and expand on what is to be accomplished and how to accomplish it.

This concept and these questions come at the beginning of the book because they create a frame of mind while you continue exploring the chapters. Along the way, *do not* lose sight of your goals and *do* execute on what you have concluded are the most appropriate ideas to pursue.

- What do those *specific goals* look like?
- Discuss them with relevant staff members.
- What is the expected benefit (for the guest and eatery), and the estimated cost and time to complete each?
- Prioritize the goals based on greatest need, including any "quick wins":
  - Be mindful of the amount of rigor placed in the decision-making process. Some ideas will require a fair amount of time to decide, whereas others could be determined quickly. A new policy for monitoring menu cleanliness is very different from implementing a new point of sale (POS) system, for example.
  - Imagine each goal having been accomplished and *visualize it* in operation. Think of the steps required to attain this goal by working backwards from the future.

- Is the goal quantifiable and being measured? Are the measurements based on historical data or industry statistics or both?
- Are they user experience (UX) related? How would it be measured?
- Create short- and long-term goals.

Never lose sight of your goals!

KNOWING YOUR AUDIENCE AND WHAT MATTERS TO THEM

Is it being greeted by a friendly host, having a friendly server, getting the meal extremely fast, having no human interaction? As the answers are unknown—because as we've seen, you don't know who will walk into your establishment—and unless the goal is to "niche down" and focus on a *particular population segment* where research and surveys have removed a lot of the guesswork, the best approach is to be prepared to handle anyone that patronizes your restaurant. Therefore, and I cannot emphasize this enough, *multiple things*, some seemingly inconsequential, must all be operating simultaneously and consistently to ensure a positive experience for *anyone* who dines in your establishment.

From the moment the guest enters the business, everything matters, from the greeter's mannerisms, the timing of server approach, food quality and so on and so forth. Depending on your goals, getting 90% correct will not get you a James Beard Award, listed in the Michelin

Guide or considered for a Michelin-star designation. Attention must be paid to *all aspects* of the restaurant, FOH *and* BOH as *both* contribute to the guest's experience. Get them right and great things can happen. But get them wrong…

STOP AND REFLECT

Besides a recipe or blueprint for how to do things, it is the *mindset* behind those decisions that is important. Think strategically, not just tactically or of the execution phase only.

- Why would customers *want* to patronize your restaurant?
- What makes it *special* or *unique* to sway the guest in its direction?
- Why is that competitor of yours clearly succeeding and exceeding the competition?
- What are *they offering* or *doing* that your restaurant is not?
- How many restaurants are within two miles and *why* would someone choose yours?

WHAT DO YOUR GUESTS WANT?

Here are the results from a non-scientific questionnaire I created asking people to rank ten possible reasons (which I specified) for visiting one restaurant over another for the *fine dining & sit-down/table service casual type of eatery*.

1. The food consistently tastes great
2. My meal is always prepared as ordered
3. The overall value (price) of my meal is good
4. Once seated, my server arrives quickly
5. The restaurant's temperature, lighting, and ambient noise level is to my liking
6. The service of food & drinks is fast
7. The portion size of my main course is good
8. The overall look & feel, décor/style of the restaurant is to my liking
9. The restrooms are clean with all available items (e.g., soap, towels)
10. Personal recognition: e.g., the staff remember me, some know my name, make me feel special

Do any of the top responses align with your answers to the "Let's get started" questions posed above?

- If yes, how do you know if these are being provided *consistently*?
- Also, did you consider the *ages* of my questionnaire respondents?

What your guests value could easily depend on their age. Depending on how your restaurant is being operated or promoted, this fact could be helping, or it could be hurting your bottom line. Unless your business is marketing towards a specific age segment, *with knowledge of what they value* and *what drives them to a restaurant*, you could be curbing your growth and possibly turning others away by being out of favor with them.

Look again at the questionnaire responses. The average age of the respondents is approximately 48. What drives this cohort to a restaurant is vastly different than diners in their 20s. For example, younger guests frequently value the ability to order a meal with minimal human interaction. Or maybe the meal value is of less concern than the importance placed on the overall experience. Ask a 60-year-old and a 22-year-old what they value in a restaurant and see the different responses. Emerging research is detailing that what drives an 18-year-old is vastly different than what would drive a 40-something-year-old. How prepared you are to handle anyone that enters your business, or if you decide to focus on a general age group, is up to you. But realize there *is a difference* in the age groups and *what* drives them.

YOUR DECIDED GOALS AND "FAILING FAST"

Do not go too far down a rabbit hole before knowing your chosen initiative will work. Be mindful that economies, environments and people's needs change, as can your restaurant's. Nothing could show this more clearly than the impact of COVID-19 on the restaurant industry.

The idea of "failing fast" involves testing an idea as quickly and cheaply as possible before investing too much money or time. You could embrace this approach to test ideas. And before tasks are undertaken, confirm they are *still* needed and, if necessary, reposition them in the hierarchy. Essentially, think crystal ball but hedge your bets with a watchful eye on the industry, trends and the behaviors displayed by your primary buying segment or bread-and-butter crowd.

MAKE SURE ALL STAFF KNOW THE GOALS

Once decided, the goals need to be known throughout the restaurant by all staff members because *everyone* needs to be singing from the same hymn sheet. To work towards the decided goals, the team must first know what those objectives are and then have them reinforced as the new approach becomes a way of life. The staff will need to know the initiatives and their importance, and management will need to echo those sentiments. If leadership and management *do not send a unified, consistent message*, initiatives will fail.

Everyone needs to be on the same page. From the owner and CEO to the busser and valet attendant. Depending on the goal, they should be communicated consistently via multiple channels wherever is appropriate—e.g.,, during shift or team meetings, on daily boards, paycheck stubs, newsletters. Think mantra.

CUSTOMER RETENTION VS. ACQUISITION

"Though they know customer retention is important, many new companies tend to focus more on customer acquisition," said *Forbes* magazine in December 2022. "I'd like to remind you that retaining a customer is much cheaper than acquiring a new customer. In fact, studies suggest that depending on the industry you are in, acquiring a new customer can cost five to seven times more than retaining an old one."

Today, it seems the customer is pickier than ever and has many options to choose from when deciding where to spend their eating-out dollars. Providing them with *what* they want *when* they want can go a long way. Here are some strategies that can help with getting and retaining customers:

- Provide excellent customer service: Meet expectations, avoid surprises and offer personalized support (see chapter 6).
- Ask for feedback: Ask customers how you are doing (see chapter 12).
- Personalize interactions: Make customers feel valued as individuals, not just numbers (see chapter 7).

- Build customer trust: Deliver what you promise and show customers that you can be relied on (see chapter 9).
- Reward customers: Make customers want to return by rewarding their loyalty (see chapter 4).

"Communication…clear, concise communication paired along with a *genuine desire* to deliver high expectations and flawless execution of product."

- Consistency in execution, be it last week, month or year.

- Have a genuine approach and connect with the guest, because they can easily tell the difference between real and fake. By keeping it real, you will get better reviews, requests and tips.

- Have your servers ask guests for a review and to mention them by name. With the increasing number of folks relying on reviews to dictate *where* they eat, the more positive reviews a restaurant can accumulate, the more likely the restaurant will benefit.

- Reward staff members who receive a five-star review!

STEPHEN SIDLO
Anthony's Coal Fired Pizza

Chapter 3

ADVERTISING &
MARKETING & USP

The restaurant's advertising and marketing efforts of how it promotes its brand, and product should align with the chosen goals and direction. Decide what they should relay. How will they draw in the potential customer? Your plans should include a focus on positive guest dining user experience practices, and if appropriate, present any unique selling points, qualities, awards or notable mentions. Conveying these can differentiate the business and help elevate and distance it from the competition. In short, you must elucidate what your company does best and *better than* the competition, with your advertising efforts coalescing around these points.

STOP AND REFLECT

How aligned are your advertising and marketing strategy dollars with what your restaurant stands for? For example:

- What is it known for (or what you *want* it to be known for)?
- What does it excel at or do better than the competition?
- Is your advertising promoting the best aspects of your business?
- Do your guests know you serve breakfast, lunch *and* dinner?

Think about your environment's distinctive qualities, and known positive characteristics, and then show them off! Brag! For example:

- The location is uniquely positioned to watch local street events or view a sunset
- The restaurant has unique art pieces, decor or paint schemes
- It has received awards or positive media write-ups for food, service, entertainment etc.
- It provides bountiful product choices—e.g., wine, liquor, seafood
- It has special seating, affording a unique dining experience

FIRST WATCH RESTAURANT
SUNRISE, FLORIDA

Garvin stays involved with his community in a number of ways.

"We are known for giving back and we've produced these wonderful 'CommUnity First' gift boxes containing such items as tumblers, coffee mugs, buy 1 get 1 free coupons and even socks with crazy designs—for example, pancakes and waffles! Depending on who the recipients are we will customize the box contents. I am very engaging and frequently speak with my guests. Many times, they'll divulge what they do or where they work. And this can result in a discussion that ultimately leads to the donation of our gift boxes. My company provides us with the tools that allow us to give back to our local community and, as such, we have donated boxes to schools, new homeowners, hotels and our repeat guests."

GARVIN MOISE
First Watch

The recipient-geared contents, or swag, proves a win–win not only for the guest, but for Garvin and First Watch as it creates positive buzz around the restaurant and the likelihood of repeat and new business! What a great practice and way to give back locally…where it matters most!

INSPIRATION: TRUE FOOD KITCHEN
LENOX SQUARE MALL, ATLANTA, GEORGIA

Stephen took advantage of the eatery's prime, visible location in the third-largest mall in Georgia and advertised on its front wall. In addition, he capitalized on events occurring at the mall. For example, during the AJC Peachtree Road Race 10K, which attracts 60,000 participants and approximately 150,000 observers, he added tables outside with a view of the course, offering complimentary snacks and beverages.

DOC B'S
INTERNATIONAL PLAZA & BAY STREET MALL, TAMPA, FLORIDA

On the mall's *restaurant row* with no less than 25 eateries, the guest needs to walk hundreds of yards from the valet to get to Doc B's Restaurant & Bar entrance while passing restaurants and bars on both sides. So how did Stephen set the restaurant apart in such an environment amongst so many competitors? Well, let's take a look.

Capturing foot traffic is the goal. Customers are going to the mall but may not know where they want to eat. Stephen started by ensuring the restaurant exterior was worthy, capturing attention with its aesthetics and clean foliage. During peak hours, he placed an employee outside with restaurant and menu knowledge and armed with miniature portions of full-size menu items to pass out as samples. For example, they will divide a full-size burger into four pieces to provide a *true* item representation and pass them out as free samples.

But the kicker was, Stephen placed this person *and the free tasty samples* near the *beginning of the trek,* near the valet, to immediately get their attention and to guide them to the eatery.

In addition, he also placed people in front of the restaurant with the instructions to greet the passersby with a simple hello and possible menu presentation...just a human interaction in an area otherwise devoid of anything personal. These tactics have worked well, with proven results including those from the guest interactions alone, so the restaurant still uses them even though Stephen works somewhere else now.

STEPHEN SIDLO
Now at Anthony's Coal Fired Pizza

It is great to see how Stephen recognizes these opportunities—dare I say it, *thinks outside of the box*—and takes full advantage of them, almost guaranteeing additional business and at the least providing inexpensive advertising *directly* to the dining public.

MAASS & ITS MICHELIN-STARRED CHEF'S COUNTER
FORT LAUDERDALE, FLORIDA

"The Chef's Counter at MAASS offers a truly unique experience where the entire kitchen is open, which allows our guests a front-row seat into all of the action. In the region, we are the only one that cooks the entire meal, plates the food right out front and then presents it directly to the guest...the *only* one. To provide more accessibility to our guests, we offer multiple experiences with different price points and menu items. Many of these items will *only be found* at the Chef's Counter and not in the dining room or even within the South Florida dining market. It truly provides a unique experience with unique cuisine. For our non-counter guests, our restaurant seating affords views of the Atlantic Ocean located directly across the street.

I've seen sushi counters and omakase counters, but nothing like MAASS' Chef's Counter. It creates a personal connection with the chef—and not just the head chef, but all of the chefs. It is important for our guests to interact with and have enjoyable conversation with all of the chefs that have contributed to preparing their meals. And this is why we have really leaned into creating an unforgettable experience at our Chef's Counter with our marketing that highlights it and our immersive menus that change weekly as well as our hosting of exclusive special-producer winery and menu pairing events. Occasionally, we will even bring in chefs from different states, cities and even countries, that, in turn, brings us press features and storytelling that results in a much greater outreach than just our local market.

We position ourselves with national publications as well as the local magazines in the Fort Lauderdale and Miami markets. And we don't just focus on the Chef's Counter but MAASS as a whole. We also stay connected by our active involvement with VisitLauderdale, a community-driven brand that celebrates the destination's diverse, vibrant and cosmopolitan region, and our involvement with the ever-popular Fort Lauderdale International Boat Show (FLIBS)."

TOBIAS FROEHLICH
MAASS

LAKE WORTH BEACH STREET PAINTING FESTIVAL

In 2024, I attended a street painting event in Lake Worth Beach, Florida, where the city closed off multiple streets to vehicular traffic to allow artists to transform the street surfaces into temporary, painted works of art. This also allowed the public to wander around the multi-block event and secure front-row restaurant seats to watch all the action. The winners were the restaurants that knew of the upcoming event and took full advantage of this two-day opportunity. One really stood out.

I witnessed Lilo's Streetfood & Bar expand their outdoor seating; create a printed, event-specific, reduced options menu; provide a temporary outside bar; set up a temporary, strategically placed host stand; and schedule increased staff. This told me that management was well aware of the upcoming event and knew how they could best use it to their and the guests' advantage.

CASE STUDY

Lilo's Streetfood & Bar

Lake Worth Beach, Florida

- Event draws roughly 300,000 citizens over its two days
- This is Lilo's ninth year participating
- There are ten restaurants in the immediate area
- Determine how to get 10% of that business:

  - Ten percent = 30,000 diners
  - How to maximize seating inside & outside
  - How to efficiently prepare meals and serve them quickly

Lindsay and the management and restaurant staff have worked this event for many years and have gained vast experience. They begin planning each year's event by reviewing historical data, including best practices and lessons learned, to see how they can successfully replicate years past and simultaneously, in the current year, increase the number of guests served.

They reserve a full-sized refrigerated and freezer-equipped truck from their primary supplier to be parked near the restaurant during the event weekend. This allows them the required storage, which their in-house walk-ins could never accommodate. They have also learned to examine the type and number of menu items, to control spoilage and to increase kitchen and server efficiency. However, they do not substitute fresh for frozen pre-packaged convenience. Nor do they stray from certain menu items that are popular and for which they are known. They simply select items that will work best for the conditions at hand without jeopardizing what makes them popular in the first place.

They have learned a lot by offering a limited menu:

- They choose menu items that the kitchen can quickly produce

  - This allows a reduction (combining) of their operating kitchen stations from five to three, as they do not need to handle as many different items

- ▢ It also allows a doubling up of the chefs assigned to each station, to produce meals more quickly and efficiently

- They produce a laminated, weekend-specific, one-page, one-sided menu
- With less menu items to choose from, guests need less time to make their selections
- Servers can focus on fewer items and be able to speak with greater authority
- Combined, these changes enable the restaurant to produce a faster table turn rate

The team has additional proven practices they put in place to improve restaurant efficiency, restaurant throughput and some just for fun!

- Locate a host stand outside of the restaurant that can more easily handle the crowds
- Add additional outside, sectioned-off seating to the side of the entrance
- Add two additional bars outside of the restaurant for takeout food and drinks
- Use walkie-talkies for convenient communication among specific staff members
- Ramp up staff with existing team members that possess prior street fair experience
- Strategically arrange their section assignments by the strength of their servers

- Bring on an additional runner/bar back
- Have costumed bartenders produce colorful fairy-tale theme drinks with edible flowers
- Have event-specific dress requirements to easily locate staff: food runners wear red hats, hosts wear red shirts, and the remaining staff wear black
- Have a DJ at the end of the event to capture the remaining townsfolk as the weekend winds down

The processes that Lindsay and her team have established, and that have been proven to work, all lead to a win–win outcome when combined. The guest is presented with a painless process for getting sat, or to grab a meal or drink on the run. The restaurant experiences a wonderful uptick in revenue for the month while simultaneously introducing itself and making a positive impact on a large number of potential future guests!

Lindsay also runs a few other restaurants, which take advantage of similar location-specific opportunities:

BRK Republic Tap House & Dog Park

West Palm Beach, Florida

A unique bar offering a selection of craft beers on tap and cocktails, plus a 5,800-sq.-ft. outdoor dog park

- Hosts an annual beer fest with the profits from the 300 tickets sold benefitting dog-focused charities

- Local distilleries and breweries donate product samples and are prominently featured at the bar, where full-sized offerings are available
- By taking advantage of an adjacent parking lot, they can host numerous specialty events
- They frequently walk around their district and offer free day dog park passes to people walking their dogs

Lucky's Gay Bar & Club Lucky

West Palm Beach, Florida

A vibrant establishment that offers a welcoming and inclusive atmosphere

- For city events such as Pride on The Block, St Patrick's Day and other annual happenings, they add outdoor seating and hire extra staff
- On Valentine's Day they host an "Ice Cream Social"

Lantern Local Tavern

Lantana, Florida

Neighborhood restaurant and bar with billiards room

- They seek out football watch groups and host events
- Based around these teams, they curate unique menus and dishes from their respective hometowns.

For example, for Chicago Bears, think Deep Dish Pizza or Chicago Hotdogs or, for New England Patriots, Lobster with Gatorade!

- They create an environment where guests can truly immerse themselves in the game while eating the team's signature dish and possibly even reminiscing about home...

For BRK, Lucky's and Lantern, Lindsay and team have consistently figured out ways to separate themselves from the competition and take advantage of a temporary set of circumstances to the direct benefit of the guest and the business.

LINDSAY LIPOVICH-MOTT
Managing Owner

BILLY'S STONE CRAB RESTAURANT AND FISHERIES
HOLLYWOOD BEACH, FLORIDA

What makes Billy's Stone Crab so unforgettable and unique is that it truly offers the best of both worlds. Upstairs, you step into refined elegance—white linen tablecloths, thoughtfully curated decor and panoramic views of the Intracoastal Waterway framed by floor-to-ceiling windows. It is romantic, elevated and designed for those moments that deserve to feel special. The continued parade of boats of every size on the Intracoastal Waterway provides unending eye candy!

Then, just below, it is a completely different energy. The downstairs dining space, including over 65ft of dockside seating, offers a casual, vibrant atmosphere filled with motion, laughter and the kind of Hollywood charm that makes you want to linger just a little longer, look at the tarpon in the water and be dazzled with the shimmery waters of the Intracoastal! Whether you are fresh off your yacht or out for sunset cocktails and a bite to eat, Billy's is the place to be. And with two environments under the same roof featuring a similar menu, Billy's can provide greater dining options when guests are pondering their next outing. Billy's unique location directly on the Intracoastal Waterway gives the guest daily front-row seats to breathtaking sunsets and a sense of peace and harmony that wraps around every dining experience.

Elena made sure those golden-hour moments were captured and shared—through polished photos on social media, elegant spreads in stylish publications and videos that make you feel like you are already there. Every ad, every post, tells a story—one of beauty, ease and connection. "Come by boat, by car or Uber and have our world famous stone crabs. You can even have them delivered overnight, by FedEx, or to your family's doorstep so they can get a peek into your Billy's experience!"

Whether the customer wants the relaxed buzz of Billy's dockside Market & Bar or the romance of the upstairs dining room, Billy's always has a table—and captivating moments to remember.

Having been founded in 1975, Billy's Stone Crab is a well-known South Florida restaurant and a respected authority in the seafood industry. So much so that it was used as an actual restaurant in a fictional book—just flip to page 29 of the action novel *Kill Washington* by David Haynes! Over the years, the Greater Fort Lauderdale Convention & Visitors Bureau has awarded Billy's Stone Crab, as well as a few individual employees, their "SUNsational Service Award." These are given to those in Broward County who go beyond in providing exceptional service to visitors. It represents excellence in the hospitality industry.

Well done Billy's!

As Billy's Stone Crab is deeply connected to the sea and appreciates its ecosystem's fragility, Billy's was also one of the first restaurants to earn the "Ocean Friendly" designation. This certification recognizes businesses that voluntarily adopt environmentally friendly practices, such as limiting the use of single-use plastics and sourcing sustainable seafood, while promoting sustainability overall. One practice they put in place was to swap out existing, harmful to-go containers and utensils with ones that are friendly to the environment.

ELENA HERSHEY
Billy's Stone Crab

I wish more restaurants would follow suit!

Billy's unique location offers something many guests clamor for, and not just in South Florida, and that is waterfront dining. So, it makes perfect sense that Elena ensured she got this message out, accompanied by quality photo and video content, across multiple outlets. She also reminds her guests that they are open for business seven days a week.

In addition, she would advertise their awards and media mentions via her social media outlets, as well as display them appropriately in the restaurant, to remind their guests of their commitment to the environment and that they had rock stars in the family.

We see unique selling positions being described in how these restaurants advertise. These establishments take advantage of their locations by consistently marketing their very desirable locations. Highlighting repeatedly what you know your guests desire is an absolute must!

MAKE THE MOST OF STRENGTHS

I know of a high-end steakhouse chain that serves USDA Prime steaks alongside non-prime cuts. The United States Department of Agriculture (USDA) has three grades of beef commonly found in restaurants: select, choice and prime, which is the best. This chain brings attention to its Prime offerings via a couple of sentences on the website and *maybe* (depending on the city) printed on menus. I mention this because the chain takes the time to call out the fact that only a very, very small percentage of steaks (roughly 3-5%) are graded USDA Prime but seems to largely ignore this fact on the printed menu, in social media posts and in conversations with the servers themselves (from my experiences). Again, 3-5% of steaks are graded Prime, and few steakhouses offer them. So why is this unique offering not more exploited in postings and server suggestions considering the increased flavor and quality of such a limited availability option?

MAASS AND THE CHEF'S COUNTER BEING AWARDED THE MICHELIN STAR

Tobias reminisces about how "immensely powerful, emotional, and unforgettable" the feeling was for staff when they realized they had been awarded the first Michelin-star in Fort Lauderdale and all of Broward County Florida.

"We just came off one of the busiest Decembers we've ever worked. January and February were also super busy. But then, the Michelin-star notification comes through…and we found out that we won! At that moment, all of the hard work paid off for each of the staff members.

The Counter was full that night. The team and our guests watched and celebrated together! The Chef de Cuisine, our number two, was in the house. Chef Ryan Ratino, the Head Chef, was in Orlando at the awards ceremony. They Face Timed him while he was on the stage!

Though we weren't certain we would win any Michelin award; to be safe, we had a Methuselah-sized bottle of champaign donated and at the ready! Needless to say, that got popped on the spot and we celebrated and included every guest in the restaurant! The Executive Chef, David Brito, was also in Orlando. Vinh Nguyen, our Chef de Cuisine, gave a speech to the staff, as did I.

Any staff that weren't working that night came in to celebrate for all the hard work that went into achieving that pinnacle award. It was truly an amazing moment. And though we were not chasing awards, it sure feels nice to be awarded."

TOBIAS FROEHLICH
MAASS

REMEMBER YOUR WEBSITE

In today's world, a restaurant's online presence is imperative. And, at a minimum, a modern, easy-to-navigate, *up-to-date* website is essential. Depending on the type of restaurant and its goals, a website should contain the following information:

- The presence of "calls to action" that align with your goals. Do you want visitors to make a table reservation, order online, purchase a gift card? Whatever the goals are, make sure it is painfully easy for the guest to navigate to and achieve those actions. For example, if your priority is table reservations, then create an obvious "Reserve Your Table Here" link/button on the home page; other examples are "Order Your Meal Here" or "Purchase Gift Card Here"
- A current breakfast, lunch, dinner, bar and happy hour menu(s)
- *High-quality photos* and possibly videos of the eatery's unique or distinctive qualities, food items and drinks. These photos should be appropriately located on the site's pages to visually represent the accompanying content—i.e., don't have all the photos only in the "photo" section
- Frequently asked questions (FAQs), About and Dining guidelines sections
- The location's address, phone number, email, directions and map segment
- Confirm that search engines are providing accurate information.

The website for *The Flagstaff House* in Boulder, Colorado, is a good example: It incorporates a website's many requirements but also captures the spirit and feeling of what one could expect while dining at this high-end establishment. The team presents the viewer with evocative images to bring them into their mountaintop home and produce a feeling of excitement and anticipation for what lies ahead.

USE SOCIAL MEDIA CONSISTENTLY

Social media management is the ongoing process of creating and scheduling content designed to grow and nurture an audience across social media platforms. While not quite producing an immediate response or call to action (CTA), the goal is to influence the viewer's decision-making to ultimately choose *your* establishment over your competitors. Social media management includes, but is not limited to:

- Social media content strategy
- Online reputation management:

  □ Ideally, respond to online negative comments or reviews within 24 hours. They should *never be deleted,* but responded to professionally.
  □ The responder should seek to understand what occurred, attempt to provide an explanation *without minimizing* the impact on the guest, all the while being empathetic. The goal is to win the guest's trust back to have them want to return to the restaurant. With the right approach, a negative experience can quickly become a positive one.
  □ At the same time, *positive* comments or reviews should be recognized!

- Community management and programming

STOP AND REFLECT

Does *your* restaurant have qualities that it brags about, are displayed on its website and frequently appear in social media postings?

Garvin believes a restaurant's presence is *"very important...10 out of 10."*

Guests *"eat with their eyes before they eat with their mouth.* Before they visit us, they like to see what to expect. We make sure our website offers great photos of each menu item."

GARVIN MOISE
First Watch

First Watch does a great job of presenting each menu item with a mouth-watering photo. They highlight seasonal offerings, drink specials, juices, iced coffee options...wherever they want to draw attention. And they do it with great photographs. Being a company that promotes freshness and healthier options, each menu item also provides the nutrition panel, which is very helpful for those concerned with food allergies or who just like reading the fine print.

> "How to flip the perfect pancake: This is just one competition that we have to bring the team together for a fun time and of course we capture all the action! I also ensure that some memorable photos and videos find their way to social media posts so our guests can join in on the fun.
>
> Another way I include our guests is by having my servers present them with a QR code to provide a review of their experience. This is invaluable in helping us keep a finger on the (guest) pulse to continue doing a great job or to correct any missteps that may have occurred. And though First Watch corporate will provide swag for these review competitions, I will sweeten the (prize) pot a little more for my team.
>
> Once, for a juice sales competition, my winning server walked away with a 55" television! That was a great day for my teammate and simultaneously, a win for my store."
>
> **GARVIN MOISE**
> First Watch

For Elena, "Billy's online presence isn't just important, it's *majorly important.*"

"In today's world, if you're not communicating with your guests online, you're invisible. That's why I've always believed that our digital platforms should be as warm, inviting, and unforgettable as walking through the doors of Billy's itself. From our website to daily social media posts, we use every channel to connect, engage and *tell our story*. Whether it is showcasing our dreamy waterfront views, a golden Florida sunset, or a jaw-dropping seafood platter straight from our boats to your table—every post is curated with intention.

We don't just post for the sake of posting. If there's a meaningful local event, a quirky national holiday, or even just a mood in the air, we'll theme our content to reflect it. It keeps things fresh, alive, and most importantly, human. I also *track everything*. I live in the insights tab. Numbers tell stories too—and if something isn't landing the way it should, I pivot. I test calls to action (CTAs) like asking our followers to say a secret word to their server. If they do, then they are gifted with a complimentary slice of our legendary Key Lime Pie. That way, we know exactly who's tuning in and more importantly, we get to make them smile.

We love to gently remind our guests through every social post and story that *Billy's* is here, ready to welcome them with open arms and water views. No need to wonder where to take your husband to celebrate a big win at work…No guessing where to toast that successful closed deal sealed with style…Or where to find that comforting, soul-soothing meal that feels like home—right on the water. At Billy's, the answer is always yes. For me, it is not just marketing, it's hospitality in the digital world. And at Billy's, we do both with heart."

ELENA HERSHEY
Billy's Stone Crab

"ONLINE PRESENCE IS EVERYTHING THESE DAYS."

"Applications exist today that can allow restaurant operations to pull their online reviews from various sources such as Yelp, OpenTable, Grubhub, Glass Door, into one platform for management to view and respond more easily. A good leader should spend 5–10 minutes every day reviewing and responding to each review be it a five-star or a one-star. We always thank the guests for the review, and we tell them that we look forward to seeing them again. And if it is a negative review, we let them know we'd like the opportunity to discuss their experience, and we provide our complete contact information as we need to earn back their trust. We encourage our servers to ask their guests for a review and to be mentioned by name and we will even provide them a free meal for every 5-star review they receive."

STEPHEN SIDLO
Anthony's Coal Fired Pizza

Today, "It is particularly important but depends on location and restaurant type."

For MAASS it is especially important, as "we have a lot of competition in the Fort Lauderdale area on the beach and with the hotels. We want to show up at the top when searching in this area. However, in Washington, DC, our sister restaurant Bresca, a one-Michelin-star restaurant, is not as important because a lot of new restaurants are opened weekly in a more crowded restaurant scene and an online restaurant presence that is over-saturated. They then dominate and capture the online presence with the most views and the press cycles. It's hard to get noticed. And a greater number of luxury and Michelin-starred ones. So, word of mouth is still the number one builder for restaurants. It's more influential. When someone tells another about a wonderful experience they've had, it holds a lot more weight than simply reading a five-star review.

One strategy that MAASS uses to spread positive word of mouth reviews is with the assistance of our 'Magic Maker.' It's a position within Hive Hospitality, Magic Maker, whose job is to create an amazing, special experience, not just a good one—make something happen that you will not find in any other restaurant. Those experiences that you've never seen, that is what gets the guest really talking to their friends and families! When they say 'that was the best experience I've ever had' versus just good food, service, and a great experience…but the *best* experience they've ever had, *that* is what is achieved with our Magic Maker and that's what I'm talking about.

Because the Magic Makers work on very tight timelines, the server is empowered to learn something about their guest. Once the server has captured this newfound information, they will inform the Magic Maker, who could also interact with the guest to gain even more knowledge before creating something incredibly special. Truly over and above! One time, our server found out a guest's favorite sweet is Krispy Kreme® donuts, and we learned this early in their meal. The Magic Maker, after discussing with the chef, made a MAASS version of a Krispy Kreme donut in a MAASS-branded Krispy Kreme-shaped box and presented it to the guest as a surprise!

Our online presence strategies are platform dependent. For example, on Instagram we're very mindful of what's trending. We like to introduce our team members by interviewing them to make them more personable, emotional and trying to connect on the human side. Whereas our Google game plan is different. On Google, we focus on our Michelin-star award and the strategies to help our rankings. We also confirm that our other awards are recognized in the area and that our Michelin-star status is clearly present. Another point on Google is that making a connection with the guest in the restaurant creates a more personable experience. And these appear to translate to more reviews where many of our servers are mentioned by name and with those increases in reviews, we will increase our ranking. The higher review scores also increase our desirability when our potential guests are online deciding where to dine. The higher the review score, the more it influences and drives the traffic."

TOBIAS FROEHLICH
MAASS

A frequent practice among restaurants is to provide a benefit, or discount, to specific segments of the population. Build My Burgers Orlando is a fitting example of this practice. It gives 50% off to police officers, a free hamburger once a month to University of Central Florida (UCF) students, and free drinks to delivery drivers, e.g., Uber Eats, even when they are not picking up food! As these drivers are delivering for the restaurant and representing and talking about their brand, Build My Burgers is generating extremely lost-cost marketing!

People rely more on social media outlets for their information needs, with eateries being no exception. Some are intentional searches while others may be happenstance. From ratings, reviews and stunning food photos to daily specials or events, your potential guest is seeing your information while they scour the internet to find that unique place in a particular part of town or simply because they have a specific cuisine in mind. It is imperative that your business postings are current and accurate, display your best qualities, highlight awards and stay in alignment with the established goals. Again, think positive UX and USP. Aside from (hopefully) presenting great photos and videos, the postings should incite a desire to patronize your restaurant.

Prior accomplishments, previously advertised or not, can be recycled by occasionally feeding them into the media stream. If the eatery was awarded or noted for something that is just as relevant today as it was in the past, it should be included in the strategy. People can have short memories. Reminding them how great something is, only makes smart business sense.

Consider bringing the guest into the decision-making process to create a sense of ownership and possibly loyalty towards the restaurant. Take

Restaurant Brands International's marketing of one of its restaurants, Burger King, and how it included guests in the process.

Burger King's Royal Perks loyalty program members can submit their spin on the signature burger, the Whopper. Guests can let their imaginations run wild and enter the Million Dollar Whopper Contest, submitting the ingredients for their dream Whopper sandwich for a chance at a $1 million prize and seeing their creation sold in restaurants nationwide. They can choose up to eight toppings that allow each guest to play out the iconic slogan to "have it your way." Since its debut in 1957, BK has created its own iterations, from the Angry Whopper to the Ghost Pepper Whopper. Now BK is turning to its guests: let their imaginations run wild—produce ideas.

"Burger King is all about Having It Your Way, and this contest is a true embodiment of that," Pat O'Toole, Burger King's CMO, said in a statement. "More than 50% of guests customize their Whopper sandwich, and now, the possibilities of what those customizations include are endless."

When asked, most people like to provide an opinion. What better way to gain loyalty than by *sincerely* seeking your guests' opinions on things that could directly impact them and the restaurant? Now imagine if you moved forward with their suggestion. Think about the positive effects, free advertising and certainly bragging rights for the winner that could be achieved!

UNIQUE SELLING POINTS (USP)

Highlight unique seating that puts the guest in the middle of the action.

Maass, Fort Lauderdale, Florida

Maass, Fort Lauderdale, Florida

Showcase your restaurant's high-end offerings.

Maass, Fort Lauderdale, Florida

Highlight the restaurant's awards.

Maass, Fort Lauderdale, Florida

Point out the restaurant's beach proximity location.

Maass, Fort Lauderdale, Florida

Play up the restaurant's directly-on-the-beach location.

Sea Level Restaurant, Fort Lauderdale Marriott Harbor Beach Resort & Spa

Sea Level Restaurant, Fort Lauderdale Marriott Harbor Beach Resort & Spa

Sea Level Restaurant, Fort Lauderdale Marriott Harbor Beach Resort & Spa

Emphasize the restaurant's waterfront location and fabulous outdoor seating.

Kaluz Restaurant, Fort Lauderdale, Florida

Kaluz Restaurant, Fort Lauderdale, Florida

Kaluz Restaurant, Fort Lauderdale, Florida

Emphasize the restaurant's waterfront location and great views from all sections.

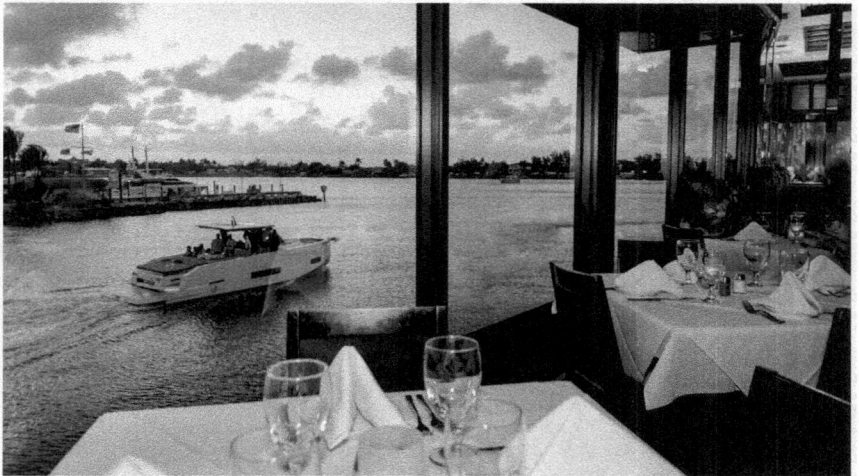

Billy's Stone Crab, Hollywood, Florida

Billy's Stone Crab, Hollywood, Florida

Billy's Stone Crab, Hollywood, Florida

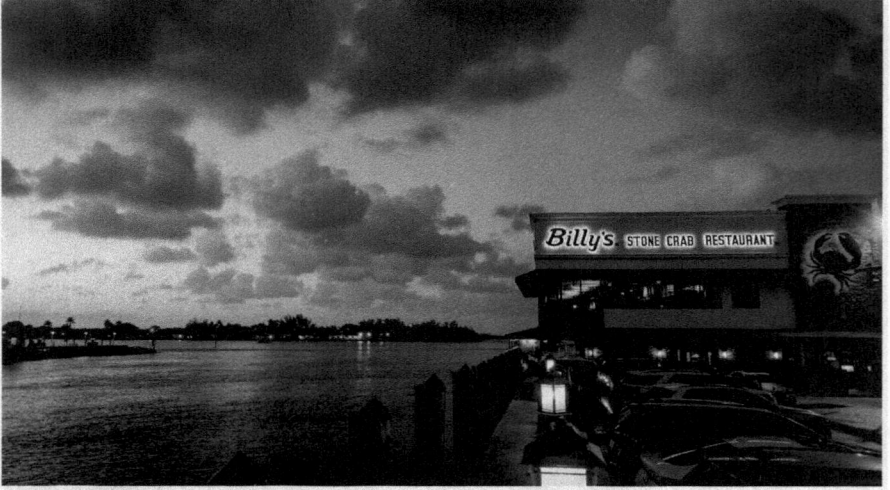

Billy's Stone Crab, Hollywood, Florida

Chapter 4

LOYALTY PROGRAMS

According to Rachel Wolff, "more restaurant chains [are] turning to loyalty programs to boost customer acquisition and encourage existing consumers to up their spending."[7] The main advantage of a loyalty program may be its most obvious one—it can help your restaurant retain customers. On both an emotional and financial level, these programs give customers a reason to keep coming back, which can be great for your bottom line. In addition, the restaurant can track what the customer ordered, when they ordered it and at which location, all of which can be used to further refine a program or promotion. Personally, I've been exposed to loyalty programs from fine dining steakhouse chains to QSRs. They can provide rewards, discounts, free perks, free

---

7   'Restaurants double down on loyalty programs to retain customers, maximize revenues', EMARKETER, March 2022. https://www.emarketer.com/content/restaurants-double-down-on-loyalty-programs-retain-customers-maximize-revenues

birthday dessert and advanced notice of upcoming specials. And I do find myself becoming loyal to the ones where I dine. The trick is to actively manage your program to ensure its achieving its targets. Having a loyalty program just for the sake of having one makes no sense. But by actively managing it and tracking the results via its multiple channels, you can adjust the offerings to better align with both the guests' and the business's aims. What's working and what's not?

From Lettuce Entertain You Restaurants'[8] "Frequent Diner Club" to a privately owned local diner, loyalty programs are clearly a great idea to attract and retain customers.

According to an analysis by Deloitte in 2022,[9] "the typical loyalty member belongs to more than one program—29% have joined two, and 38% belong to three or more. Almost half (47%) use their loyalty memberships several times a month, and almost a third (32%) do so several times a week."

ENCOURAGE DIRECT ORDERS

Food aggregators, or food delivery aggregators, are third-party companies that offer a single online platform for handling restaurant meal ordering, delivery and customer service. Think Uber Eats, DoorDash, Grubhub. Numerous studies have shown that orders placed online tend to have final checks up to 20% higher, on average, than those placed in-house. By balancing the cost/pricing equation, these third-party services can provide additional restaurant awareness and some profits. But unless

---

8   Lettuce Entertain You Enterprises, Inc., the largest privately held restaurant group in the US with roughly 50 unique restaurant brands.

9   *Unlocking the value of loyalty programs for restaurants: Serving up new opportunities to build customer loyalty.* https://www.deloitte.com/us/en/Industries/consumer/articles/restaurant-loyalty-program.html

the restaurant increases its prices, it will absolutely see reduced profits from orders placed through the Uber Eats and Postmates of the world. In addition, guest metrics are mostly absent when the customer orders directly from the aggregator.

Instead, invest in an online ordering system and content management system (CMS) with ordering, POS integration etc., and direct the client to your own website and not to an aggregator. *Make it obvious* that they will save money by ordering directly from you (and ensure your prices are indeed lower). Ensure a quality photo representing each menu food item is standard practice. A third-party will still provide the delivery component, but now the guest has ordered from "X" restaurant and not "DoorDash." And best of all, metrics can be captured to use for future direct marketing and loyalty program changes.

Below, I am providing bullet points of information based on a study,[10] to illustrate the importance of aggregators and the direct impact they can have on your business. Rather than summarizing their work, I've simply taken sections directly from their document that complement our discussions on providing the best guest experience. Keep in mind that the surveys were conducted immediately following the COVID-19 pandemic. Much has changed since 2022, though much value lies within and remains in these findings.

"We surveyed a panel of 501 managers from restaurants across the United States in September 2021 about the ordering, payment and fulfillment features their businesses offer and the innovations in which they plan to invest for a glimpse into their innovation strategies. We also

---

10   The February 2022 edition of *The Restaurant Friction Index*, by PYMNTS Intelligence (www.pymnts.com) https://www.pymnts.com/wp-content/uploads/2022/02/PYMNTS-Restaurant-Friction-Index-February-2022.pdf

surveyed a census-balanced panel of 2,146 U.S. consumers in October 2021 about their restaurant-ordering habits.

- Nearly all restaurants use loyalty programs to encourage consumers to order directly from the restaurant by offering discounts on menu items. Forty-one percent of consumers say loyalty programs would encourage them to purchase from restaurants.

- The average restaurant prices their items 4% lower for loyalty program members than for the average website customer, offering cost-conscious consumers a way to dodge high price tags. In total, 96% of all restaurants mark down prices for loyalty program members.

- Other features that consumers say would encourage them to make more purchases from restaurants include the ability to pay and order online and the ability to pick up food orders via drive-thru and curbside.

- Our research shows that 40% of consumers would be more likely to order from restaurants that allowed them to pay or order online, for example, and 33% would be more likely to order from restaurants from which they could pick up curbside.

- Just 57% of all restaurants currently offer loyalty and rewards programs, for example, and 25% plan to invest in them in the next three years.

- Chain QSRs offer more ordering and fulfillment options than other eateries.

- Chain QSRs are the most likely type of restaurant to allow customers to order via mobile app, aggregator and loyalty channel.

- We found that 96% of chain QSRs allow customers to order via aggregator and mobile app, while 76% allow ordering through a loyalty channel.
- Restaurants now receive orders through an average of 2.7 different purchasing channels at any given time. Consumers place these orders via mobile app, aggregator, desktop website, on-site visits or over the phone. *One impact of this development is that more sales now are generated through digital channels than either on-site or over the phone.*
- PYMNTS' data shows that 41% of the average restaurant's sales now come through digital channels such as mobile apps, aggregators and websites. This share of sales is far more than the 32% the average restaurant generated via its brick-and-mortar location and the 26% generated via phone call.
- Providing a highly integrated cross-channel ordering experience is key to driving sales in the digital-first restaurant industry.
- Restaurants charge an average of 24% more for menu items listed on aggregators than for the same items listed on their own websites.
- QSRs are the most likely restaurant type to bump up their aggregator prices, with 27% of QSR managers confirming that they sell the same foods for higher prices on aggregators than they do on their websites. Just 14% of table-service restaurant managers do the same."

PART II

ACHIEVING EXCELLENT USER EXPERIENCE

Chapter 5

RESTAURANT MANAGERS—LEADERS

The managers (leaders) should stay in communication throughout shifts to discuss any information that affects guests. To keep abreast of customers' experience, management should interact with patrons during breakfast, lunch and dinner services to ensure the restaurant is delivering on what they've vowed—i.e., a great guest experience. Keeping with the book's areas of focus, we'll view these management (leader) positions through the lens of their impact on the UX and/or USP.

I am referring to these positions as manager-leader because they require attributes from both titles to accomplish greatness. Aside from ensuring daily operations run smoothly and goals are being met, these positions champion the business's vision and strategic direction and communicate both effectively.

To further increase the business's level of success, I believe in leadership "shadowing" key positions in the restaurant, *especially* when they have no firsthand knowledge of a role. By spending time following an experienced team member, the leader can gain enlightening and invaluable understanding. Their ability to relate to their employees increases exponentially as they've "been there, done that!"

> "Walk a mile in their shoes."

Furthermore, leaders that attend training courses on topics such as conflict resolution, communication tactics, mentoring and strategic thinking will be better prepared to perform their job and more effective when working with others.

FRONT OF HOUSE (FOH) MANAGER-LEADER

The front of house manager will supervise the entire FOH team. They'll provide team leadership, monitor and manage customer service satisfaction, arrange staff training and ensure an excellent restaurant flow between the FOH and the BOH. In addition, they will monitor and manage the ambiance and work with the general manager to ensure the customer is being well taken care of.

STOP AND REFLECT

Manager Awareness:

- What are you *seeing?*
- What are you *hearing?*
- Allocate enough time to guest observation and engagement
- Allocate enough time to staff observation and *their* guest engagement
- Are the restrooms clean *and* adequately stocked?
- Are the room temperature, lighting and sound levels acceptable?

BACK OF HOUSE (BOH) MANAGER-LEADER

The BOH manager is responsible for managing the BOH staff and operations, including the kitchen, dry and cold storage and dishwashing. Supply ordering, inventory, health regulations, staff hiring, training and scheduling could also fall under their watch. If a head chef (aka kitchen manager) exists, they would work closely with them.

Maintaining a clean BOH is a critical responsibility of this position, because deficiencies in this area can have devastating effects on the restaurant's reputation. Any failed inspections from the health department can quickly surface on the local news and social media outlets. And once it appears on someone's Facebook feed, it can spread like wildfire. The resultant consequence for the eatery's reputation could be life-changing for the business. And if the restaurant were to be shut down for any length of time, it runs the risk of losing existing customers and being unable to acquire new ones.

It is understood that food preparation is a necessary part of the kitchen duties:

- In advance, the staff is juicing oranges, creating biscuit mix, cracking eggs, quartering chickens, marinating meats, chopping vegetables, creating dressings and sauces, filling numerous stainless steel food bins on the line...all to ensure availability of needed items for the staff.
- Checklists for the morning and afternoon crews can assist in ensuring all prep work gets completed, stays consistent and operates in a systematic way.
- All stored prepped items should be dated and rotated, for example, using FIFO (first in, first out) to ensure freshness and safety and to minimize waste.
- Knowing which dishes are popular (via POS reports or purchase tracking) can assist in determining the quantities of ingredients necessary to be prepped.
- Using report data showing which dishes sell, during what shift and on what days, can assist purchasing in stocking the necessary items. This will also lead to less waste and a smaller chance of depleting inventory of a needed menu item.

Conversely, a lack of solid inventory management processes can have negative effects on the business. Not having needed items prepared ahead of time and the needed ingredients to create something on the fly, if necessary, could result in a delayed order or even "86-ing" something prematurely.

"Billy's did an exceptional job of inventory management and was remarkably aware of what was needed to fulfill their menu requirements. As such, Billy's prides itself on never having to "86" anything. Billy used to say: "We don't 86 at Billy's!" Make it happen!"

ELENA HERSHEY
Billy's Stone Crab

Now, if we're talking about a nightly special with limited quantities that is communicated to the guests, that is one thing. But when a standard menu item can't be prepared because of mismanagement or a delivery delay, that is something entirely different. Be mindful that your guests do not expect dishes on the printed menu to be unavailable. And some may have even patronized your restaurant for that specific dish, their go-to, their favorite as it turns out. And when it is not available, you are left with a dissatisfied customer.

What's more frustrating is when an out-of-stock item is something that can be purchased in the supermarket within the same plaza. Mind you, I realize not all eateries are enabled to carry this task out.

If a problem can be solved easily, act and fix it.

"When starting to run low on an item, Doc B's puts a "product" or "meal remaining" count in the point of sale system to notify the serving staff. They will also communicate with staff on the communication board of what's out and nearly out and ensure that each server is aware of this. The managers are responsible for telling each server the state of the menu items running low so they can communicate appropriately to the guest. So, in the event a guest orders an item that may be unavailable, the server can now respond that they'll need to check with the chef or kitchen as they were hearing this item/dish/meal was beginning to run low.

When a menu item is *known to be unavailable*, the server will explain *at the beginning* of the interaction that they have unfortunately run out of a particular item. This will alleviate anyone unknowingly ordering said item and *then having to be told* it is unavailable. Whenever possible, set expectations ahead of time."

STEPHEN SIDLO
Anthony's Coal Fired Pizza

Garvin and his team have this motto as part of the First Watch culture: "Never 86 an item!"

"We rarely, if ever, 86 a standard menu item. But, if something unforeseen occurs, we already have a plan in place! Firstly, the managers will discuss amongst themselves. Secondly, we'll list the out of stock item on our three kitchen boards to be highly visible. Thirdly, we will verbally tell each server that enters the kitchen and inform them to spread the word when out on the floor.

After we have managed the internal communications, we will attempt to source the item from a local grocery store. If that proves unsuccessful, we will contact the closest First Watch restaurants. In the event they do not have enough inventory to spare, we will procure from our closest food and equipment wholesale supplier."

GARVIN MOISE
First Watch

"It happens. Restaurants will occasionally be out of an item or ingredient even with the best of preparation. But how the realization is handled can make all the difference in the world. The longer it takes to recognize that something is out and to communicate this to the staff, the worse it becomes for the guest. So, our team is very transparent.

The staff is notified immediately if something has unexpectedly run out. The server will inform the guest right away and recommend an alternative with enthusiasm. If an alternative is not found quickly, the chef will become engaged and will visit the table. They will discuss what they can or cannot prepare and then will proceed to make something special for that guest, all the while being enthusiastic in their approach.

By being transparent, the guest appreciates it and feels very respected. They see that the restaurant didn't try to hide anything or create something of lower quality just to make a certain item. It results in very little disappointment to the guest by the way it's handled by the server, chef and management.

Occasionally, a guest may come in looking for their favorite dish at a time it happens to be unavailable. If this occurs, a manager will always get involved. They will stop by the table to provide their personal contact information, including email and telephone number. They will also inform the guest that they will receive their favorite meal, at no charge, upon their next return visit.

We do our best to avoid these situations by managing our inventory closely. Also, we will use our POS system to notify our staff when our item counts are beginning to run low and even have it place a block on an item. In addition, when we realize we have a very limited number of an item left, the food runner and managers will spread the word widely, ensuring the entire floor staff is aware."

TOBIAS FROEHLICH
MAASS

TRY NOT TO "THROTTLE" THE KITCHEN

If the kitchen is getting into the weeds because of too many tickets, a lack of staff or a high number of food aggregator orders, how do you throttle, or manage, the kitchen to allow them to catch up? And, simultaneously, keep the in-house and delivery customers satisfied *and* avoid a negative experience and review?

Honestly, it is not an easy task to manage when a restaurant experiences a rush of guests that quickly overwhelms the kitchen with a flood of tickets. When I used to host, the GM would tell us to sit any open tables if we were on a wait regardless of the effect on the server being hit with multiple parties or the impact on the kitchen. The thinking was to not delay the inevitable and simply to continue and feed the kitchen tickets.

Unfortunately, and frequently, what happens is that the kitchen gets into the weeds, the server returns to the table, apologizes and explains how the kitchen is slammed, and would they like a drink refill, and the customer begins to get aggravated. Sound familiar?

One way to reduce the impact is by communicating with the BOH staff:

- Let them know that a rush is expected at a certain time based on the reservation count.
- This should prompt them to confirm the line is adequately stocked with all necessary food items, clean cookware and dishes.
- They should also make sure the expo station is fully stocked with its needed dishes, salad-making materials, soups etc.
- The FOH manager, and any team leads, should also let the server, bus, host and bar staff know about the expected rush.
- No breaks should be authorized.
- Hosts and food runners could assist with soft drinks, water and bread service.
- Bussers should have empty tubs at their stations.
- The bar should confirm it has ice, clean glasses and empty dirty dish tubs.
- The restrooms should be verified, clean and stocked.

In other words, for a known impending rush, you should know that you've done everything possible in advance to set the restaurant up for success.

Another way to prepare for a possible rush is to reference the business's POS to view historical daily and weekly meal counts and restaurant turns (see chapter 12). These statistics will hopefully provide insight into what may lie ahead, which is why a modern POS system is essential for managing expectations, true costs, advertising dollars and myriad other items. If historical data does reveal a probable rush, communication is needed *before the start of the shift* to prepare the staff and to set off several directives. The items broken down above should be discussed at the shift meeting with any additional specifics. Think ahead. Prepare ahead.

If a problem can be solved easily, act and fix it.

HOW TO HANDLE A RUSH

If the restaurant *does* get slammed and the kitchen falls behind, it is very important for staff to maintain their composure, be cheerful and use communication as a primary tool of choice.

Have you ever noticed how *not* knowing the cause of something can be more frustrating than when you do know? Take for example a traffic jam on the highway where you have no idea if the cause is just around the bend or miles up the road. But when you *know* the cause is one mile ahead you feel better as you know when the traffic will start to flow again, and you have a confirmed end to the slowdown. Well, your guests are like the vehicles sitting on the highway, but they are looking for their meals, not when they can resume a normal driving speed.

Therefore, *communication is key* from the servers and FOH leaders to ensure the guests continue to be looked after, not ignored, and are provided timely beverage and/or bread service, and of course, timely communication of their meal's status. If the delay is determined to be egregious, and/or the server observes the guests are getting upset, the server should do everything in their allowed capacity to remedy the negative situation. The FOH manager should consider visiting the table and possibly providing something additional and/or something for a future visit.

It is management's decision to direct the hosts to sit waiting guests immediately upon a table opening up, even if it will result in a server being "multi-sat." But simply delaying each sat party by a few minutes can help stagger the tickets entering the kitchen and may take some of the edge off. In addition, it wouldn't hurt to forewarn the guests if, in fact, the kitchen is starting to struggle, that the meals may take a little longer than normal. Again, set expectations *ahead of time*.

For the food delivery aggregators or guest pickup, set *realistic expectations*. It is better to present a realistic time for delivery or pickup than to over-promise, deliver the order late and create a negative experience. By being transparent and giving realistic delivery times, even if the guest may not be happy with the response if it is longer than desired, you will have set accurate expectations and avoided the situation of "where in the world is our order?" AI-driven capacity management software applications can take on these duties of providing accurate, dynamic delivery and pickup times as well as give real-time or near-real-time updates.

> "For Stephen and Doc B's Restaurant, "Pacing the right way is the difference between winning and losing in the restaurant business." Sometimes he will pause seating for 5–10 minutes and go on a wait and will explain to the guest that it will allow the kitchen to get caught up and thus be able to provide a better experience for them. In the meanwhile, the guest may take this opportunity to patronize the bar, which itself proves to be a win–win outcome."

STEPHEN SIDLO
Anthony's Coal Fired Pizza

When Garvin and team find themselves in a particularly busy kitchen environment, Garvin maintains his cool:

> "I will not show that I'm stressed or feeling overwhelmed, as I believe that it can be sensed by my staff and can only exacerbate the situation. So, rather than broadcasting the state of the kitchen, I will simply pull one or all of the managers off of the floor and place them on the line as all managers at First Watch are trained to cook every meal on the menu."

GARVIN MOISE
First Watch

FOOD CONSISTENCY

This cannot be overstated. One driver of repeat business is that the guest "knows" what to expect. From the look of their favorite plated menu item to the taste of the freshly baked bread, steak seasoning, blackened fish entrée, house vinaigrette dressing, spicy shrimp appetizer, and post-meal coffee. They've eaten there. They enjoy eating there. Why is that? Well, generally speaking, the raison d'être of any eatery is the food. Therefore, once your dishes are perfected, make sure the results remain consistent. The BOH manager oversees food quality while ensuring kitchen and service staff follow food safety guidelines.

The placement and presentation of the food on the plate can have a positive or negative impact on the guest. The way the food is presented is very important and will be the first thing the diner sees. The cook and expo should be cognizant of this and ensure the food is offered in an organized and appetizing way. Granted, I would expect a fine dining eatery to possess better plating skills, but that is not always the case. And conversely, is it OK for a fast casual restaurant not to have any plating awareness? Of course not. If adding a piece of well-placed kale or a sprinkle of chopped parsley or an artistic drizzle of sauce prevents what otherwise would be a bland presentation, then do it. I'm sure you've received some austere plates in the past and thought to yourself, wow, how boring or bland the food looks.

If a problem can be solved easily, act and fix it.

COLD OR ROOM TEMPERATURE BUTTER? (ADMITTEDLY A PET PEEVE OF MINE)

Have you ever received rock-hard butter for your soft bread? How did that make you feel? Is that ever appropriate, in any type of restaurant and especially in a fine dining one? What would be needed to ensure the butter is at room temperature for the guests?

If a problem can be solved easily, act and fix it.

Chapter 6

GENERAL MANAGER (GM)—LEADER

The GM manages the entire operation—i.e., the BOH and FOH—and is the glue, or connection, between the two areas. As the go-to person, the GM is to ensure a smooth operation because they have visibility into all facets of the business. They should also interact with guests to ensure the restaurant's goals are being met and they will most likely have overlapping duties with the FOH manager. As both positions' overarching goal is to maintain a well-organized operating environment, they will be heavily invested in observing the flow of both houses and the resultant impact on the dining guest.

Some common responsibilities (*may be influenced by other restaurant roles*):

- Employee hiring, management, motivation & performance evaluations

- Guest engagement, satisfaction & complaint handling
- Creating a positive culture of support and inclusivity
- Menu creation, pricing, periodic reviewing & updating
  - *Before* printing menus, multiple people should triple-check the structure, item order, placement, photos, spacing, font size, margin size, spelling, grammar etc.

- Marketing strategies
- Supply ordering & vendor management
- Financial, safety & Health Department-related responsibilities
- Remaining current on restaurant trends
- Attempting to predict future business needs

GM awareness:

- What are you *seeing?*
- What are you *hearing?*
- Think about how to increase business
- Allocate enough time to guest observation and engagement
- Allocate enough time to staff observation and their guest engagement

CUSTOMER SATISFACTION

As the GM oversees the entire operation, they play a critical role as their actions can directly influence the diner's experience as well as the restaurant's overall financial well-being. Depending on what other management roles exist, e.g., FOH and kitchen manager, those duties would largely fall upon the GM. For this writing, let's assume these are the GM's responsibility, and for the sake of efficiency, we won't restate the aforementioned positions' duties.

Sticking with our UX/USP focus, it is incumbent on the GM to maintain an awareness of the business's daily operations, for both houses, as both can have an impact on the guest's dining experience. A breakdown in the BOH will cause a negative experience for the guest in the FOH. Is the kitchen keeping pace with the FOH? Are the guests happy and receiving their meals timely? Are there any servers in the weeds? Are there any ingredients close to running out? What mechanisms are in place to confirm both houses are in harmony, for example, receiving feedback from an expeditor, server or host with subsequent adjustments?

REDUCING WASTE AND SOCIAL RESPONSIBILITY

The National Restaurant Association's *86 Food Waste Initiative* is a set of data-driven resources highlighting actionable steps to help restaurant operators eliminate food waste. It debuted in early 2020 in partnership with the World Wildlife Fund and support of Essity and Tork.

Reading this report may help you find new practices that will help your eatery find ways to reduce waste in both the BOH and FOH, reduce costs and help the planet. In addition, depending on the specific actions taken, social media posts can be created around the positive impacts being tackled by the restaurant. A win–win!

HOW TO MAKE STAFF FEEL VALUABLE... AND IMPROVE THE BOTTOM LINE

For a restaurant to provide a total quality dining experience, it helps when the staff is included in relevant initiatives and feels valued as team contributors. This aligns with the *leader* part of the manager's title and a demonstrated environment of support, inclusivity, approachability, etc. Some restaurants go as far as making staff equity shareholders—the belief is that they will work harder when having a personal stake in the business.

Having recurring "town hall meetings" to discuss the business's goals, specifically with a focus on those that directly impact the guest, is a great start. The staff should be encouraged to share their actions taken with guests that produced positive outcomes. The idea is to share these so other team members can learn from them and apply them when appropriate. Maybe employ something akin to the North Star Strategy/ Framework (a product-based approach that helps businesses optimize their success by focusing on a single metric that reflects customer value) to help with the approach when collaborating with the staff.

The town hall meeting should also include prior initiative results and plans for future quality undertakings. As a group, the restaurant staff, FOH and BOH, should be encouraged to provide their insight from *their* experiences and their opinion on how they feel negative experiences could be best managed in the future. Don't forget to include those incidents some may consider inconsequential, because you may pick up some quick wins in the process. Ideas could be written down on sticky notes and placed into "buckets" of related items on a wall for further distillation, discussion and ranking by what the business deems most important. Ultimately, a well-defined plan should emerge based on the business's most pressing needs and should include expected completion dates, progress tracking and the expected results/value/benefits. And don't forget to make the staff feel valued with free appetizers or meals, especially because this meeting will most likely require some to attend on their days off.

"There is no real way to motivate an individual that doesn't want to be motivated." They get motivated by *your* motivation. When the managers, trainers, and leads get excited when speaking about things, then the staff can get excited. A great tactic is by touching on an emotion that the employee has experienced in their life and by harkening something back to them, they will react and get excited. All pre-shift meetings start and end with positive discussion points. Negative topics are discussed in the middle à la the *sandwich model* where one wraps a negative criticism between two positive aspects. With good success, Stephen has also employed role playing in pre-shift meetings. He will have two to three team members going through the *other team members' spiels* that *they* give to the customer. By representing each of their roles it allows them to learn from this and create comradery and a willingness to help each other as the moods have been lightened, it is fun and educational at the same time. They are getting to know each other and how *they* present themselves and their positions to the guests.

One way Stephen increases the odds of motivating his staff is how he approaches hiring at Doc B's…he will ask his stronger staff members essentially "why they choose to work there and why do they want to stay." He found that most offer the same reasons for why they remain versus looking elsewhere. Therefore, Stephen seeks to find others that *match* these reasons as they would become more of a cohesive group. His hiring is then dictated based on his better-performing team members' reasons.

He determines what motivates these team members and then builds on that to help them achieve their goals by gelling better with each other. He finds it easier to drive such exercises in a single, unified direction versus with multiple goals and motivators. He feeds whatever motivates them and why they are there and has seen where the culture can be a larger motivator than simply money.

STEPHEN SIDLO
Anthony's Coal Fired Pizza

"Coach in the moment" and "Tell, Show, Do, Show" are some tactics Garvin employs with his team. He combines these with tools presented in their onboarding virtual learning. While also possessing years of prior sales experience, Garvin will reach into his historical toolbox to assist his team when speaking with their guests on how to suggest alternatives and upsell.

"During our FOH shift meetings, I'll coach in the moment and may also execute role playing. First, I'll instruct my team on *how* to do something and then *show* them how to do it. We will also review our POS system for items that may be giving our servers issues or that they have questions about. Ultimately, I'll seek a response from my servers to confirm they understand what's being taught.

I am also a very gregarious person and frequently hold the door for our guests, engage them in conversation, call them by their names and generally treat them as friends. My servers see these interactions, which I believe rubs off on them. It has become part of our culture."

GARVIN MOISE
First Watch

Elena explains that her husband, Billy, was adept at motivating people as he was a strong and a powerful leader. Billy and Elena would conduct customer service training, led by the manager on duty, at least once weekly to motivate and fire up their staff. Daily, they would have a 15–20-minute pre-shift huddle where they would emphasize the restaurant's goals and remind staff of how to provide a WOW dining experience which would build up their confidence. The FOH *and* BOH staff would attend these meetings as Billy, Elena, managers on duty and the staff knew it was a concerted effort to achieve the exacting standards expected of them.

As detailed in the Server chapter (9) of this book, Elena would continuously train her servers on how to achieve the "wow-effect" when presenting their seafood platter to their guests. And, aside from the details of the presentation, Elena believed in showing praise to her servers. One way she would recognize those that excelled at customer service would be the opportunity to oversee larger parties. She knew these servers' personalities and that they had proven themselves adept at handling full sections and demanding situations.

ELENA HERSHEY
Billy's Stone Crab

Billy and Elena knew that by reinforcing the hard *and* soft skills necessary for the staff to excel in their positions, they would help their employees become more comfortable and confident in themselves. This would directly translate to a better experience for the guest, better gratuities for the server and better outcomes for the restaurant in the form of repeat business. A win–win–win for sure! Elena always trained her servers to put on a show to "wow" the guests.

"Billy's is a true family business, that's why I believe it stands the test of time. In 2025, Billy's Stone Crab celebrates 50 years of legacy and 30 years in the centennial city of Hollywood, FL. Many of our team members have grown with us, like Luis, who began at 16 after emigrating from Cuba and still plays a key role in the kitchen. His son JR followed him, building a thriving career at Billy's. This spirit of generational continuity lives on through many families here, passing down Billy's values, quality and integrity to the next generation."

ELENA HERSHEY
Billy's Stone Crab

STAYING THE COURSE AFTER YOU ARE AWARDED A MICHELIN-STAR

Tobias explains that winning the star is only the beginning. Maintaining it and embracing the impact come next.

"We like to celebrate the Michelin-star whenever we can and include our guests to celebrate alongside us. Once you receive the star the expectations for the restaurant will only increase. But this only motivates us to keep it up…our service, our food, our quality, our consistency…they all go up with that as well.

Besides celebrating being a star recipient, we also like to advertise it. We feature the Bibendum character (the official name of the Michelin Man) on our menu and in the restaurant. We have included it in the press, in online outlets and in as many magazines as possible. As we are the only Michelin-star restaurant in the city of Fort Lauderdale and surrounding area, we share this information through our social media accounts, newsletters and public relations outreach on a national level. We make sure that everyone knows, and the results have been obvious.

As soon as the star award came out, we experienced an immediate increase in demand and bookings. The reservations were coming in fast and furious, as experienced by the nonstop ringing of my phone. People were booking that night!

MAASS, as part of The Hive Hospitality Group (comprised of four restaurants, a cocktail bar and five total stars within the group including MAASS), is the largest of the concepts to receive a star. This is great for the brand and now makes us tied with the most renowned restaurant groups for the most Michelin stars in the United States. Tied for the most Michelin-accoladed restaurant group in the country. Hive Hospitality and Chef Ryan Ratino are becoming synonymous with fine dining and Michelin accolades!

Winning the Michelin-star has motivated us to work even harder. We realize the responsibility in accepting the star and the expectations that it brings from our guests. Each member of my team recognizes this, and they continue striving to make our guests' dining experience the absolute best they've ever had."

TOBIAS FROEHLICH
MAASS

SYNERGISTIC EFFECT OF TWO HOUSES EQUALS ONE GREAT EXPERIENCE

Understand that the front and back of house items discussed above are part of a much larger picture—that is, to serve the guest in the best conceivable way. Individually, a singular bad item may not present an overly negative experience, but multiple items, if they are not managed well, could absolutely create a negative UX and potentially one with teeth. Understand each area's responsibility in serving the customer. Understand the relationship between them. Understand that each must be actively managed. By viewing the FOH and BOH not as separate but as one unit whose team members rely on each other, your restaurant can consistently provide what your guests want…a great dining experience and one where they will be eager to return.

Chapter 7

GREETERS

This position is frequently the first one that your guests will meet when entering the restaurant. The host/greeter's appearance, personality, attitude, everything can have an impact on the guest, good or bad. In addition, during peak times, a server may request the hostess bring water or run non-alcoholic drinks to a table.

Therefore, do not overlook this critical position. As the saying goes, "you never get a second chance to make a first impression."

STOP AND REFLECT

How would you feel if you entered a restaurant, let alone an upscale one, and the host acted uninterested, or removed, when speaking with you? They made no eye contact, weren't smiling, did not speak loudly enough and simply grabbed the menus and began to walk away assuming you knew to follow them. How would that make you feel? Conversely, how would you feel if a well-dressed host greeted you with a genuine smile, maintained eye contact and spoke at an appropriate volume while welcoming you to the restaurant?

How does hosting look at your restaurant?

APPEARANCE AND DRESS CODE

As this person is typically the first to encounter the guest, they should be well groomed and free of body odor as well as heavy perfumes or colognes. Clean fingernails and neatly trimmed facial hair and an appropriate amount of personal accessories. Depending on the restaurant style (fine, casual, family style…), a specific dress code could be warranted. Perhaps uniforms. The takeaway is that the person should be dressed appropriately to match the restaurant's style and formality. Avoid clothing with messages, because they could be misconstrued. Refrain from anything too extreme. The upscale restaurant type would demand a more fashionable presentation that clearly matches the restaurant's prestige and price point. Are ties, wrinkle-free dress shirts, jackets or suits recommended for the men? Are wrinkle-free dresses, pant suits or suitably long skirts appropriate for the women? Maybe shorts, khakis or polo shirts? Only you can answer that. Any choice should include closed-toe shoes that are clean and polished. When athletic shoes are allowed, they should look clean. Of course, if it is an expensive seafood restaurant serving patrons on newspapers, the host would most likely not dress for the New York runways, but something more appropriate to that specific environment. At the end of the day, ensure your greeters' dress and appearance match the feel or vibe of the restaurant and what it is trying to portray. And if in doubt, angle towards overdressing rather than underdressing.

STOP AND REFLECT

What impression does *your* eatery want to make?

And if a team member, any team member, has memorized a customer's name, it adds much more to the experience by making the guest feel very welcomed and even special. This can alter your guest's decision-making next time they're thinking of places to dine—everyone wants to patronize a business "where everybody knows your name!" Just ask Norm from the television show *Cheers!* You get my drift. Be friendly and greet each guest with a smile. You have one chance to make a great first impression on the guest—don't blow it!

OTHER RESPONSIBILITIES

Keep in mind how each of the following is executed and *how it could impact* a guest's dining experience. Think positive UX!

- Takeout orders: The taking and/or fulfilling of phoned-in or online orders may fall to this role, and this may include the stocking of related items.
- Reservations: The greeters will manage reservations and the wait list. Many restaurants use online reservation systems to support these duties, usually with parameters entered by the eatery to control the customer flow. An example is Tock, whose new tagline *Delicious Starts Here* claims it can "sell ordinary reservations alongside unique experiences, like a chef's counter, cocktail class, or happy hour. Tock helps you drive revenue to every service."
- Determining wait times: If wait times cannot be determined automatically, most restaurants have an average occupancy time dependent on the table's seating size. Keeping an accurate time log for the tables allows for even better estimates. Typically, add an extra 10–15 minutes to avoid the guest being under-quoted.
- Host stand or counter: As this is the first area the guest will see, it needs to be kept clean and organized. In addition, the front door and waiting area should be inspected throughout the shift, ensuring they remain up to the cleanliness standards.
- Multi-greeters' scheduled shifts: With multiple hosts, the duties will be split, with each having different responsibilities. Scenarios could include: a minimum of one greeter remaining at the front door, or host stand, greeting the guests and maintaining the waitlist; with at least one host maintaining a

front door presence, two additional hosts could be responsible for splitting the restaurant and sitting their respective half; one hostess could be assisting bussers in clearing tables and then subsequently informing the main host of an open table. Most importantly, the guest must always be warmly greeted when entering the restaurant.

- Sitting a multi-section/station layout: Hosts should sit the guests in an equitable manner, allowing each server the same number of sat tables. This allows for similar earnings potential and simultaneously doesn't overburden any one server, which could negatively impact the guests' experience. While seating guests, be aware of the pace when they are led to the table. Confirm they are aware they are being sat and *always walk at the guests' pace*—do *not* charge ahead.

- Table preference: If a guest appears unhappy with the table choice or requests a change, try to accommodate the request as quickly as possible. And don't forget to inform the main host and, if one is in use, update the table management system.

- Table environment: Take a quick look-see of the table and chairs to ensure cleanliness and that it has complete table settings and remove unnecessary items.

- Server-sat awareness: The greeters should keep a mental note of seated guests and ensure that the server is aware they've been sat. If unsure, communicate directly or through a co-worker.

- Sitting incomplete parties: If the restaurant only sits complete parties, *ensure this is stated* on any online reservation platforms. In addition, if a guest calls the restaurant to book, it should be stated at that time. Knowing this ahead of time will reduce the risk of unhappy guests wondering why they aren't being sat.

- Cutting a "multi-greeter" scheduled shift: As closing time begins to draw near and the restaurant slows, hosts can be cut as the pace would no longer warrant having multiple greeters. The cut host(s) should begin any sidework and take steps to leave their space(s) in good shape for those remaining or for the next shift. The remaining host(s) will need to maintain "front door awareness" while seating new guests and potentially performing their other duties such as bathroom cleanliness checks.

- Menus: Menus must always be kept clean, and this is the responsibility of the host position. In addition, worn menus should be brought to the attention of management for possible replacement.

- Unhappy guests: Management should be notified of any unhappy guests immediately. Explain the situation to the best of your recollection.

- Miscellaneous: When not sitting guests, the host can assist in clearing and setting tables; inspecting and cleaning menus; restocking items under their watch; remaining aware of guests who may be in need.

- Guests departing restaurant: The departing guest must always be acknowledged when leaving the eatery with a friendly salutation: "Have a great day or night," "See you soon," "Thank you for coming in today or tonight". Aside from the host's responsibility, other staff members can participate.

MORE ON RESERVATIONS/TABLE MANAGEMENT/HOST APPLICATIONS

Today, options exist that make it much easier to manage reservations and tables than in times past. Some items for the staff to oversee include the following:

- Table seating chart with the ability to "see" where the table is at in the meal-consumption timeline, and the host can walk the restaurant with a touchscreen tablet computer to verify and make updates.
- When the system is integrated with the POS, the host can *see* where the diner/table is at with real-time course statuses. For example, the table is at the appetizer, main, dessert, check dropped stage. The host will then get a better sense of when the table would be available, which will provide more accurate wait time estimates.
- Automated, digital, customizable surveys can be created that collect private feedback from guests after they've completed their meals.
- With POS integration, it is possible to create dining room strategic decision reports. These reports can show the average per person spend by the party size and *reservation source*, which can ultimately assist with sales forecasting, staffing levels and advertising.

Combined, these can all lead to a better user experience as they produce a more realistic wait time estimate.

Tobias ensures the guests at MAASS, and the Chef's Counter receive exemplary service. To that end, one way he can guarantee this is by knowing every one of his teammates are qualified to fulfill most positions.

"Everyone that is hired is cross-trained and have spent days being educated in each position.

No one is 'above' performing any duty. If we find ourselves down a team member, it's simple to spread the staff out to make sure what needs to happen happens. And seeing that the guest experience is paramount, we will deprioritize other restaurant tasks to achieve this even if it means working later than anticipated. We may have a bartender seat a guest or perform dish washing. We may have a server do bus work or meal prep. And the GM can just as easily take out the trash or seat a party of five as they can provide critical support in times of need. By each of us performing each other's positions, it allows us to 'walk a mile in another person's shoes' and creates mutual respect for how difficult a position can be, and, in the end, it reinforces our team spirit. 'That's not my job' or 'that's not in my job description' doesn't fly around here.

At the end of the day 'it's all of our jobs' and it needs to happen, and we all have fun while doing it."

TOBIAS FROEHLICH
MAASS

If Billy's Stone Crab find themselves down a greeter, Elena assumes the role of hostess to maintain the level of service Billy's guests have become accustomed to.

ELENA HERSHEY
Billy's Stone Crab

"At First Watch, we truly operate as a team and have cross-trained our servers, hosts, cashiers and to-go positions. This way, we can easily cover a scheduled shift when we occasionally come up short. We also have a pool of servers that can be contacted in the event we need coverage at the front door. And they will also be provided with a free shift meal. I also have the possibility of 'borrowing' a greeter from a nearby First Watch, which is made painless due to our operational systems capabilities."

GARVIN MOISE
First Watch

How great is that! Servers, hosts and the to-go person all cross-trained. Talk about coverage!

When Doc B's are busy and find themselves short-staffed on hosts, they know what to do; they pivot. And that's a good thing because since the COVID-19 pandemic, it's proven more challenging to retain staff and they more often have to work with less experienced staff. If Stephen is unable to pull in additional resources, he will move people around and put his "aces in places." He will put his head manager at the greet stand, knowing the current condition of the wait, who can steer the guest with the appropriate messaging and simultaneously provide the best pace to the restaurant.

PACING THE RESTAURANT (KITCHEN) STRATEGY

Stephen will have only one walker (host) take guests to a table. But that single host, by default, will dictate the pace of orders, the number and timing of tickets hitting the kitchen, the servers not getting slammed...all of which equates to a good dining experience. By keeping a greeter always staffed at the front, and taking the guest's name, they can explain that their host is seating someone and will be back in a moment to take them to their table. This ensures a more moderate submission pace of kitchen tickets and service bar orders without placing them in the weeds.

While walking, they'll also have a conversation about anything with the guests...nice shoes, nice weather, have you eaten here before. The topic of discussion is less important than simply talking to the guest while walking them to their table. They will be warm and welcoming. Also, talking to the host keeps the guests' focus on them rather than on any open tables. However, if they want to change tables, the host will inform them that they would love to accommodate them, but they'll need to walk back to the host stand to follow up with the host coordinator. The beauty of this tactic is that upon hearing this, it puts the decision-making in the guest's hands. A percent of guests will simply accept the original table and for those that will not, it buys the servers and kitchen a few minutes to catch up without additional meals being ordered and tickets generated. The host is still providing the pace. For major holidays and known busy days, Stephen will have his most experienced host or manager run the door to absolutely control the pace of the eatery.

STEPHEN SIDLO
Anthony's Coal Fired Pizza

These are splendid examples of how the hosts can positively impact a guest's dining experience by virtue of how they can impact the kitchen. Each role in the restaurant plays a part in ensuring the houses run smoothly and the diners have a wonderful dining experience.

Chapter 8

BAR

A bartender's personality, and their rapport with customers, as well as any signature or wow-factor drinks, can positively impact the bar business.

For guests that like friendly bartenders who remember their name, what they drink and other personal points, this could easily sway them to patronize that bar over another. Again, think user experience. The guest feels welcomed, as if they are seeing a "friend." The more personable and genuine the bartender, the tighter the relationship and greater the chance for repeat business.

STOP AND REFLECT

Signature drinks, eye-catching ones and those that exhibit a wow-factor response can likely have the guest clamoring for their cell phone camera! And what comes next? The photo is uploaded to a social media site accompanied by the restaurant's name and other photos of the guests having a fun time at *your* restaurant! For free! How many drinks does your bar produce that elicit such a response? They chose your bar for a reason. So, provide them a reason to spread the word, or photos!

FUNCTION OF THE BAR

Bars may be located in the front of house (FOH) and can incorporate the service bar for the servers to fill drink orders. They can also be in the back of house (BOH) as purely a service bar. Service bars can be very utilitarian, because the diners will have no interaction with this operation. Other things being equal, thought should still be put into the layout and location of the BOH service bar. They should be conveniently located for the servers to place and retrieve their drink orders without blocking traffic between the two houses. The layout should include enough surface space for prepared drinks to be logically organized and placed for quick identification and retrieval from the server.

Depending on the restaurant's license, the bar may serve hard liquor, beer or wine. The bar may serve no food, limited food items or the complete restaurant menu. The bar may have its own drink and food specials apart from the restaurant's main dining area. The bar may contain high-tops, booths or standard-height tables and have reserved seating, open seating or a combination of the two. The bar may have a bountiful wine, scotch, bourbon, tequila or beer product selection. The bar may offer unique, hard-to-get and seasonal product offerings. The bar size, type, product offerings and overall makeup are up to the business to decide.

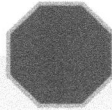

STOP AND REFLECT

What are the goals for the bar's existence? Is it to drive traffic to itself, or to the restaurant or to both? Is there an expectation to achieve a specific profit margin?

PLANNING A BEVERAGE PROGRAM

Some of these questions may be answered by producing a beverage program. Percentages can vary by restaurant but beverage sales, if priced appropriately compared to their *pour cost*, can produce a good profit margin. Conversely, if pour costs are *not* managed appropriately, the profit margin could drop substantially. Creating a beverage program to manage the business's bar and drink service can be an asset and increase the bottom line.

What liquor brands, varieties and drinks do you or will you offer? Aside from *ensuring the pour costs and profit margins are in alignment with the business's goals and restaurant type*, management should "listen" and get to know their customers' buying patterns.

- What are they ordering?
- Which of the stocked liquors and beer aren't selling?
- Speak to the servers and bartenders, who are close to the guest, to understand firsthand what is being requested
- If you are not offering what the buying customer is asking for, why not?
- If a problem can be solved easily, act and fix it

Once you know what alcohols and drinks to provide, the next step is to set the pricing.

- The price offered can be appropriate to the type of restaurant—i.e., a high-end eatery would likely charge more than a casual one for the same item
- Wine has a higher average pour cost than beer and liquor and should be monitored more closely for cost changes
- When can items be priced higher and when can they be priced lower? Guests know when they are getting a good or fair deal

  □ For example: *Veuve Clicquot Yellow Label Brut Champagne 750ml* is $50–60 at your local liquor store. I know of a fine dining restaurant in South Florida that advertises a price of $165, which is easily three times the cost. Conversely, I know of a fine dining steak house chain with a more traditional price of $135 and a seafood chain with a very moderately priced bottle at $89

Some estimates put the total restaurant beverage sales averages at 25–30% of the overall sales numbers. I believe a more important metric would be the known pour cost of those sales. Industry standard pour costs are between 18% and 24% and this is what restaurants usually target. Breaking this down further, we get roughly 28% for wine, beer 24% and 15% for liquor. So before tackling a plan to increase the beverage sale percentages, first, you need to implement a plan to manage the pour costs. A software application, or POS add-on, would be the most convenient path to enter all liquor costs, broken down by unit cost—e.g., one 12-ounce bottle of beer; 1.5- or 2-ounce liquor pour broken down by each unit bottle; a glass of wine. Of course, all the accompanying items such as mixers and garnishments used for each drink need to be added to the system to gain a more accurate figure.

Extensive wine lists and matched offerings, or pairings, to menu items are additional ways to increase the bottom line. A bartender offering suggested pairings when a guest orders food is a great value-add and appreciated. *Servers in the main dining area should also employ the same tactic.* Of course, the menu could also display pairing suggestions. Alcohol-free cocktails or mocktails should be included with any drink offering, because many people are forgoing the alcohol but still like the "drink experience." Offering freshly brewed quality coffee is another easy offering and one that can add to the bottom line while creating a positive guest dining experience.

REMEMBER TO MONITOR PROGRESS

Once the beverage program has been created, it is important to track the soundness of the decisions made and to monitor all pour costs. Key performance indicators (KPIs) should be identified and consistently reviewed as part of the business's standard operations to confirm items such as pour costs, what's selling, what's not selling, the return on the advertising spend, drink special sales, etc. As prices can easily change over a brief period of time, what once was a profitable drink offering can quickly be reduced to one barely breaking even or worse.

Determine an *accurate* pour cost. Price drinks accordingly and then the two (cost and price) *must be monitored.*

Chapter 9

SERVER

The wait staff function as the primary liaison between the diners and the kitchen and play a pivotal role throughout a guest's dining experience. Their extensive knowledge of the menu, combined with their professionalism, positive personality and service quality, significantly shape and enhance the overall affair. They should be friendly, genuine and engaging, and should try to build rapport. Remember, the folks that patronize your restaurant could eat at home. But instead, they've decided to go out to eat at *your* restaurant and they ended up in "your" section.

Today, the dining public is looking more for an experience when they dine out. Fine dining guests have even extended their average dining time to get their money's worth in today's economy. And you had better believe that that experience is expected to be a positive one! Their reason for deciding to dine out is irrelevant. Maybe they are simply having a long day and didn't want to cook. Maybe they have friends in town or are celebrating a special occasion. *Whatever* the reason they decided to dine out, they are expecting to have an enjoyable time. Period. End of story. It is *your* job to make this a reality!

At First Watch, Garvin takes comfort in knowing that all new employees, FOH and BOH, complete over eight hours of structured training. They must complete all assigned onboarding assignments for their continued employment. This encompasses virtual learning, scenario-based and in-house training and covers a multitude of topics such as food safety handling and passing the state food handler exam, harassment, seating and, of course, customer service.

Their "Five Steps of Service" breaks down some fundamentals of providing great service and covers items like the greeting and getting the order correct the first time. In fact, the restaurant and corporate office monitor all employees' training for completion and adherence. First Watch's training regimen lays the foundation for a smoother guest experience by preparing the staff to offer a great experience from the get-go and of course covers how to better handle any issues if they arise.

Garvin reminds his staff to remain watchful for the "Meerkat Guest!" In a meerkat social group (a "mob") the meerkat sentinel duty is a behavior where one or more meerkats act as lookouts, scanning the environment for predators like birds of prey, jackals or snakes. Now, in First Watch you'll never see any jackals or snakes, but you may see a guest looking for assistance. Thus, Garvin and staff are always looking for "meerkats!" Can't you see them? Sitting upright, head swiveling from side to side waiting to catch the server's or someone's attention.

GARVIN MOISE
First Watch

BILLY'S STONE CRAB'S SIGNATURE SEAFOOD PLATTER: A STORY WORTH SAVORING

"With a name like *Billy's Stone Crab Restaurant and Fisheries*, seafood isn't just a menu item—it is the soul of the experience. That's why Elena made it a point to turn their Signature Seafood Platter into more than just a dish… it is a moment, a memory and a story.

Every server at Billy's is trained not just to serve—but to *present*—their ocean treasures with flair and intention. The platter arrives meticulously curated, each element placed with precision, highlighting the freshness and vibrancy of the sea and the boldness of the top-quality meat.

But here's where it gets magical: the team doesn't just describe the items—they *tell the story*. A story of sea-to-table excellence, of their very own fisheries and dedicated fleet in the Florida Keys, which ensures every crab, lobster, shrimp and South Florida fish arrives with freshness, and unmatched flavor.

And of course, there's the beautiful detail about their star—the stone crab. A true renewable delicacy. Guests learn that only the legal-sized claws are harvested, and the crab is returned to the ocean, where it regenerates its claws within 12 to 24 months. It is sustainability in action, and the guests love knowing that what they're enjoying is both luxurious and responsible. "It is more than dinner; it's a *wow moment*—and every one of our guests deserves nothing less."

ELENA HERSHEY
Billy's Stone Crab

At Doc B's, Stephen has trained his servers to set expectations of cook times that are *longer than usually expected* of specific dishes, by informing the guest ahead of time and furthermore, asking them if that is ok—e.g., saying it will take 18–20 minutes to prepare a particular fried chicken dish. By incorporating this tactic, his servers set the expectation of a meal arriving *later than one is accustomed to,* which thereby removes any question as to "where is my meal?" They were informed ahead of time!

STEPHEN SIDLO
Anthony's Coal Fired Pizza

And, as I've previously stated, "If a problem can be solved easily, act and fix it." Well, Stephen has done just that.

The guest's experience begins the moment they enter the restaurant, where they've potentially already interacted with a valet, door person and host before being greeted by the server. Ideally, the server should approach the table within one minute of the guest being seated.

One practice I have witnessed is that the host places a ticket, or index card, on the table in the shape of a tent to signify they have yet to be approached by the server. A host or other team member may notice and follow up by informing the server that they've been sat. If the ticket is flat, it reveals that someone *has approached* the table and possibly taken a drink order.

> "If Billy's know they will be down a server, and they can't fill that shift, the size of the station is reduced. And though this practice reduces the number of meals served and profits for that day, it is much more important to maintain the quality and the integrity of service their guests expect. Another tactic is to offer meal service at the bar if their stronger team of bartenders are working, as management know they can handle the extra responsibility flawlessly."

> **ELENA HERSHEY**
> Billy's Stone Crab

> "When Doc B's finds themselves short-staffed on servers, they will close certain sections rather than overloading the remaining ones, which could surely lead to a reduced dining experience. Simultaneously, they try to make this less obvious, so guests don't see unseated tables while the restaurant is on a waitlist."

> **STEPHEN SIDLO**
> Anthony's Coal Fired Pizza

Whereas some restaurants would continue to seat sections with more than the recommended number of guests, I agree with Elena's and Stephen's approach, which protects the guest from receiving a poor dining experience and protects the restaurant from receiving negative reviews and creating unhappy servers.

ORDER TAKING AND IDENTIFYING SEATING POSITIONS

Identifying *who* ordered *what* is particularly important, especially in high-end eateries. I am assuming most POS applications will track meals ordered information with a corresponding table number, but this number would need to equate to a table seating position that the restaurant staff understand. Besides the server, this will allow any person who is running food to accurately place the meals, especially if the restaurant has an open hands practice. Unless it is acceptable for a team member to approach the table and yell out "who had the New York Strip?" it is best to know where the food should be placed.

OPENING WINE

Present the bottle to the guest who ordered it to confirm it is correct. Then, use a waiter's corkscrew that can easily be maneuvered while holding the bottle in your hands *rather than resting it on the table* to begin opening the bottle. Remove the foil under the *lower lip* by using the corkscrew's knife. Here, a serrated blade works best. Then insert the screw part, or worm, into the cork and screw about halfway down. Position the corkscrew lever over the lip of the bottle, and while holding the wine bottle and the lever firmly, use the main part of the corkscrew to pull the cork out of the bottle while earning bonus points by keeping the label facing the guest who placed the order. Place the cork on the table in front of the guest. Pour a small amount into *their* wine glass and wait for the acceptance or rejection of the wine. With approval, fill each glass on the table and *finish with* the guest who ordered the bottle.

If the wine chosen is rejected by the guest for a technical issue such as a bad smell, rotten cork or other obvious defect, the restaurant should replace the bottle without resistance. Outside of an issue with the wine itself, it is at the restaurant's discretion on how they would handle the return of an apparently good bottle of wine.

STOP AND REFLECT

Keep in mind how the following could impact the guests' dining experience. Think UX.

- Glassware cleanliness
  - No one wants to get a water-stained glass or one with lipstick residue

- Communicate meal progress
  - As mentioned in the Managers chapter (5), the guests should be kept apprised of their meal status when exceeding the standard timeline

- Time to approach table after meals are dropped
  - Have you ever been approached by the server after your meal has arrived to see how "everything is looking or tasting," yet you haven't begun eating? Don't do that!

       ☐ Give the guest a chance to *begin* eating their meals before approaching them to confirm it is to their liking

- Beverage refills
  - ☐ In the United States, the beverages go on the right side above the flatware, thus, refills should occur from the right side

- Glassware handling and etiquette
  - ☐ Do not remove the refillable beverage from the table. Instead, refill it at the table or bring a fresh one
  - ☐ Do not grab the glass at the top from where the guest drinks

- Meal delivery
  - ☐ Do not bring only *some* of the table's meals—i.e., a partial order. Hold meals in the back and/or have a team member assist with the delivery

- Dirty dish removal etiquette
  - ☐ Traditionally, in America, food items are presented to the guest from the left while dirty dishes are removed from the right
  - ☐ Ask before taking any plate, even empty ones
  - ☐ In general, it's best practice to wait until *all guests* at the table have finished eating before clearing the course's dishes, especially in formal dining settings. Clearing *one* guest's dish before the others may make their companions feel uncomfortable and rushed to finish *their* meals
  - ☐ Never cross an arm in front of the guest

- Coffee, dessert, digestifs (after dinner drinks)
  - ☐ Offering these items can place the finishing touches on the evening's experience. Suggesting a fresh cup of coffee, or after-meal drink, may be exactly what the guest wants but wasn't necessarily thinking about. Calling out some of the restaurant's most popular dessert items could be another potential win and could pair wonderfully with the drinks. Of course, these added items are a triple-win for the guest, server and the restaurant!

CUTTING SERVERS

As closing time begins to draw near and the restaurant slows, servers are typically "cut" and told to end their shift. At that time, they will finish servicing their sat tables and begin any sidework. Their stations will be "absorbed" by the remaining servers in an equitable manner—i.e., tables are divided between them, to avoid overburdening one server and to keep the earning potential on an equal footing.

UNHAPPY GUESTS

Whenever a guest appears unhappy, the server should always initiate a conversation to determine the cause. It is important that the server stay aware of the guests' mood and behavior for possible clues that something is amiss. And if in fact something is bothering the guest, hopefully it is something minor that the server can remedy. I know people that will not reveal anything to the server or manager when they've had an unpleasant experience. And they would not return and might even talk badly about the restaurant. They'd *rather not deal with a discussion about why they aren't happy.*

It is not always easy to see when a guest is unhappy, which makes staying "tuned in" to the diners important. If a problem exists that the server cannot fix, they should inform their manager immediately and provide them with as much information as possible. Precisely how the manager attempts to "correct" the situation, I cannot answer. But I know that they should approach the guest with humility and present themselves as extremely genuine in how they propose to "fix" whatever made the guest unhappy. If they handle this well, an unpleasant situation can disappear, with the guest possibly recounting to friends how the manager went out of their way to ensure they were satisfied. A win–win. Conversely, if the manager handles this poorly…

At Billy's, they don't shy away from feedback—they *welcome* it. Whether it is a comment from a guest, a less-than-glowing review online, or something Elena personally witnesses in the dining room, they treat every moment as an opportunity to get better, sharper and more aligned with their standard of excellence.

If a guest voices a concern or leaves a critical review, Elena explains that the management team jumps on it *immediately* and that they don't let things sit. "We review the situation, then bring it to our daily training huddle where we walk through what happened and how we can elevate the experience next time. At Billy's the manager on duty is brought to the table and the guest is offered either a complimentary drink, dessert, a gift card or the check is adjusted."

Elena believes in coaching, not criticizing. She'll often say, "This isn't about blame and pointing fingers at who did what wrong. It is about togetherness and us making things better and more efficient." We break down real scenarios, role-play different presentations and empower our team with the tools to turn a potentially negative moment into one that wins the guest over. This builds trust and loyalty with the customer. Billy would always say: "A customer's trust has to be earned every day—it is not a given."

ELENA HERSHEY
Billy's Stone Crab

I couldn't agree more with Billy's expression...

How you train your staff to manage dissatisfied guests can make all the difference in the world. Because they've spent most of the time with the guests, ensure they know how to ask the right questions and how to propose the best solution. Instead of the server immediately seeking a manager, as part of his onboarding and training, Stephen personally educates his servers and validates any trainers' instructions and approach for best practices. He makes certain his employees are comfortable when communicating with the guest under such circumstances to ensure a positive outcome for managing an unhappy guest. Stephen reviews with his staff what they are authorized to provide without seeking a manager's approval. Ideally this will lead to a happy guest with the manager simply paying a subsequent visit to the table to lend additional empathy and possibly provide something extra to send them off with, thus, really showing that the restaurant values them as a guest.

STEPHEN SIDLO
Anthony's Coal Fired Pizza

"One of the most important things, especially in the restaurant business, is how to train your staff in turning around a negative guest experience. It's critically important as it's in real time, person to person, face-to-face.

- Listen first. Let the guest explain. They want to be heard…I am making sure we listen.

- We highlight the issue and resolve it immediately.

- I have empowered the staff to resolve issues.

- They're instructed first to speak with the chef to immediately make any necessary changes. Whatever needs to happen, make it happen.

- The manager will always visit the table to ensure the guest is satisfied and that they leave happy and with positive memories.

I see guest complaints as opportunities, because when guests are unhappy, we usually correct the situation, turn them around and they become some of our most loyal regular customers.

We gave them the attention that they deserved and made sure they had a good time and that they felt very well taken care of. Traditionally, these same guests have returned countless times where we continue to take great care of them!

These times also present themselves as huge opportunities in that you can either fail to right a wrong, at which point they will never return. Or you can show them what you're made of, go over and above to rectify the situation and, in turn, you become one of their favorite spots.

It's a huge opportunity because after we turn them around…we've created a fan for life.

How well has it worked out at MAASS?

> The results have been excellent! For example, just tonight a couple is returning for the more luxurious experience at the Chef's Counter. Unfortunately, their first experience wasn't as good as the restaurant would like, so we invited them to return.
>
> Originally, the server had sensed it, proceeded to make it better and then had the manager stop by. But it still wasn't the best recovery. So, we contacted them within a few days, and the conversation went very well and tonight will be their seventh visit!
>
> Overall, the results have been truly positive, with the staff being very receptive and embracing our best practices for ensuring none of our guests have anything less than a great dining experience."

TOBIAS FROEHLICH
MAASS

Chapter 10

FOOD RUNNER

The primary responsibility of the food runner, or runner, is to transport food items from the kitchen to all tables, in all sections unless otherwise decided by management. Primarily it would be the appetizers and the main dishes, and it could also include running items to the bar. They may run complete or partial orders and can also accompany a server that is carrying additional items. The runner may also be asked to bring single items to a table at any time during the guests' visit. Traditionally, the runner will present the food items from the guest's left side. And if they need to remove a dirty dish, they will remove it from the right.

Though not required, a ticket that indicates which seating position a meal corresponds to will alleviate the food presenter (whether the runner or server) from having to ask the table "who ordered the prime rib?" In fancier restaurants, this is usually protocol. Personally, I would expect this in a fine dining establishment.

The runner should ensure that the guest has everything required at the time of food delivery. They should quickly confirm all necessary plates, flatware, steak knives and napkins are in order, and ask the table if anything additional is needed. This will relieve the server of overseeing this task and ensure a better user experience. If a guest requests something from the runner, the runner should respond accordingly, depending on their position's allowed duties. Regardless of whether the runner can directly accommodate the request, they should inform the guest that they will handle it or will handle it by informing their server.

When the food runner is picking up the order from the kitchen window or "pass," they should quickly assess the condition of the physical dishes to ensure nothing is chipped or dirty. They should also view the table ticket and confirm all add-ons such as bullets, or ramekins, of sauces on the side have been included, and which expected garnishments have been added. (If an expeditor is in place, they should cover these final items.)

EXPEDITOR "EXPO"

The expeditor or expo organizes a ticket's prepared food items and sends them out when the ticket is complete. As the cooks complete the dishes, they are placed in the window or on the shelf (the pass), where the expo will begin to group them while ensuring completeness. They will potentially add garnishments to the dishes, clean any plate edges to improve their appearance, confirm there are no chips or existing dirty food remnants and will ultimately deem the order complete to be run to the guests' table.

Typically, the line will call out its own orders—i.e., the cook will instruct the others of what dishes to begin, how many and when. Occasionally, the expediter may be missing an item from a ticket and will communicate to the cook that something needs to be "fired" to complete the ticket. However, in other restaurants, the expo may control the ticket intake and feeding of information to the line. They would be responsible for juggling the timing of the dish "firing," knowing that dishes have varied cooking times and ideally all should be finished simultaneously. In addition, they will need to assess what each cook is currently working on, to avoid placing them "in the weeds."

STOP AND REFLECT

When an order must be made "on the fly," it is important that the expo gives this dish priority. Typically, when something is made urgently, outside of the meals presented on the original ticket, it is frequently because an original dish was not accepted by the guest and was returned. In this case, the remaining members at the guest's table may have their meals and could be waiting for this replacement meal to arrive. And the person waiting could insist that everyone else "go ahead and eat." Either way, it is not an enjoyable experience for any guest at the table. Therefore, if a dish needs to be replaced, it should essentially leap-frog the other tickets to make that table whole or complete.

Just like the dishwasher, the expediter and food runner play important roles, and they can impact the guest experience because they interact with patrons at critical times of the dining experience. By ensuring the meals are prepared correctly, include all requested items, are served on clean plates, are presented correctly and at the same time and then confirming that nothing additional is needed, together, they can provide a wonderful experience.

Chapter 11

DISHWASHER

The primary responsibility of a dishwasher is to ensure a continuous supply of clean items. They must be certain everything is cleaned thoroughly from the FOH—e.g., tableware items such as dishes, glasses and flatware. In addition, they must ensure the kitchen staff has an adequate supply of clean BOH items such as pots, pans, spatulas, ladles, spoons, tongs and cooking sheets. Whatever items are consumed by the line need to always be available. Restocking the line, expeditor, soup and salad stations with appropriate items would be expected, as would general kitchen cleaning duties. Note that the bus staff may fulfill some restocking duties.

Keeping a continuous supply of FOH items for the kitchen is paramount for the kitchen to perform its job in a productive and efficient manner. Without clean kitchen cookware and utensils, the cooks cannot provide a complete food dish. Without clean dishes, they cannot plate the food.

The FOH bussing station is usually tended to by the busser, but the dishwasher may also transport the dirty dish tubs to their BOH area while simultaneously replacing them with clean tubs. This ensures a faster process for removing unwanted items from the guests' table and thus improving their experience.

Stocking the FOH or BOH bar is another area the dishwasher, and possibly a busser, may assist with. Depending on whether a barback exists, the dishwasher may assist in removing dirty dishes and glass tubs while replacing them with new clean ones, restocking dishes, glasses, flatware, condiments, ice and any other non-alcoholic items. Whatever items are consumed by the bar(s) need to always be available.

The dishwasher should keep an eye out and remove items from circulation that are unsightly or damaged, such as chipped plates, glasses, ceramic sauce cups (ramekins) and overly worn flatware. If the overall condition of any of these item groups is beginning to show its age, the dishwasher should bring it to the attention of the kitchen manager for possible replacement.

If a To-Go Area exists, the dishwasher may be responsible for maintaining all necessary items to package orders—e.g., bags, containers, disposable flatware, paper napkins, individual sauce packets, paper menus. These restocking duties may be the responsibility of the person staffing this station or the bus staff.

STOP AND REFLECT

The role of the dishwasher should not be understated when it comes to providing your guests with the best experience.

Have you ever received a broken or chipped plate or glass? What about lipstick- or water-stained glassware? Or flatware that looked like it had been used for five years? How did that make you feel and what impression did it provide of the restaurant? Now, imagine how your guests feel and what that says about the restaurant.

Recollect what I have previously stated: the restaurant staff, *all staff* work as a team to ultimately provide an exceptional guest user experience. It truly *is* a team effort. By keeping the bus stations clean and available for accepting dirty dishes; by removing damaged, less than spotless tableware; by ensuring a continuous supply of needed kitchen and bar items…all of this leads to a smoother running operation and one that will ensure a better guest experience as each restaurant staff member can perform *their* job better.

The dishwasher's importance, and how they contribute to the overall restaurant experience, should be communicated and reinforced with the people in this role. Remember that in times of need, *everyone* chips in. If you are not busy, and you see another person is, lend a hand to assist them!

Chapter 12

POINT OF
SALE SYSTEM

Tracking dish popularity to better manage and respond to customer preferences; easy access to inventory levels, allowing for replenishment precisely when needed; viewing robust historical and period sales data. These are just some ways point of sale (POS) systems have revolutionized how restaurants are managed. The central component of your information technology stack *begins* with the point of sale system. Beyond the application's initial cost, the ROI of a robust POS can improve sales, operational effectiveness, and help minimize waste by tighter inventory tracking. We are not going to delve into all the details and features of a POS' capabilities. Rather, we will focus on the main aspects that could affect customers' experiences while dining at your eatery.

GUEST BEHAVIOR AND FEEDBACK

Your POS shows you what people buy and where they buy it—in the restaurant, in the bar, from aggregators... You can see what's popular—and what's not. Assess what you see and make changes if necessary and appropriate. Is there something you often sell out of? Maybe it's worth keeping more in stock, to reduce the risk of disappointing anyone who wants to order it. But remain mindful of its cost and how it is priced.

Watch out for changes in tastes, too—don't keep stocking items that people no longer want.

You also have feedback in the form of verbal complaints or thanks, as well as formal surveys. Consider this feedback regularly alongside the POS data and your overall goals, to assess whether you are still delivering the intended UX.

TRACKING GOALS

How do you know if the business's goals are being met? Are they being tracked? Keep an eye on your overall goals *as well as what customers want.*

Aside from the mandated collection and retention of certain data, collecting information without viewing it is a valueless effort. One can collect an enormous amount of data but without its timely review, it is not providing value. Even "real-time data" is historical by nature—it tells you what has occurred in the past. Thus, data's timely review is essential to use it in the most productive ways. In other words, *don't collect data for the sake of collecting data.*

We've already stated the importance of using historical data in earlier chapters. But what data is the most critical to the restaurant's financial health, guest experience and the maintaining and acquisition of sales?

The specific metrics you need will be unique to your restaurant, but in general, the following data collected via a POS would be a good starting place:

- All food and bar items' cost
- All methods of food sale generation—e.g., delivery and delivery provider, online, telephone
- All in-house dining, takeout, drive-thru sales segments
- All guest survey outlets

STOP AND REFLECT

By closely tracking food and bar costs, the eatery can make informed pricing changes. These can be based on things such as the restaurant's perceived value by the customer, its history, uniqueness and comparison to regional and local related competitors. Costs can go up but increasing prices correspondingly is not a foregone conclusion.

Could another item be offset? Could something else be offered for free or increased in value or perceived value? What is the best way to juggle increased costs while avoiding an overly negative reaction to a price increase?

Understanding from *where* an item is sold will assist in determining menu pricing, and thankfully, the POS has already captured this data. As we know, price points vary and are set differently depending on the sales channel—e.g., in-house vs. food delivery aggregator. As such, tracking all purchases, and knowing the "where," will assist in making the appropriate price changes.

Utilizing guest opinion surveys via an in-house method, or by other means, can provide valuable data. Customer response reports from sources such as Resy, OpenTable, the company's website, printed check receipt website link or digital payment screen can provide direct, timely feedback.

Suggestions

- If recommended tip amounts are offered, the percentages should be based on the *pretax* amount.
- When automatically adding a gratuity for large parties, or for any reason, ensure this information is *plainly visible* on the check.
- Add a survey QR code and link to printed check receipts. The survey should be brief, with no more than five *concisely written* questions with a radio button and/or check-box. response formats. Think carefully about the survey content, focusing responses on the most pressing business questions. Include a free-text comment section, so that people can also give feedback in their own words.
- Monitoring all survey channels is an assigned task. Any negative responses should be escalated to leadership, and a response is provided, preferably within 24 hours. Responding to positive reviews is also recommended. Positive comments that call out staff members should be communicated directly to them as well as during any team or town hall meetings. Spread the great news!
- Consider providing something of perceived value in exchange for survey responses.

Chapter 13

RESTROOMS

Did you decide that they do, or they do not? And more importantly, how did you draw that conclusion? Do you think a message is sent subliminally to the guest when they enter either an exceptionally clean, well-stocked restroom, or conversely a messy one that is not fully stocked?

To me, the state of an eatery's restroom speaks volumes.

When I encounter an obviously well-tended one that is lacking nothing, I know that management has made its importance clear to the team and additionally made it a responsibility of a specific position or positions. The hosts and bussers would be tasked with verifying the restrooms are up to the set standards. Furthermore, these confirmations would be on a set schedule. They understand that a negative message is sent to the guest who enters an ignored restroom, and they make it a point to see that that does not occur.

And aside from the frustration experienced when there are no paper towels, I cannot help but think that management may be lacking rigor in more impactful areas if there is no hand soap.

What do you think when you enter a restroom that has overflowing trash receptacles, dirty paper towels on the floor, standing water on the sink vanity? It speaks volumes about management practices.

Unfortunately, I seldom find bathrooms today that *check all the boxes—* so much so that when I *do* come across them, I consciously think "wow, they've done it right." Management realizes the positive message it sends, and has communicated this to the staff, who are clearly following suit. They want to provide a positive guest experience and do not want it to be jeopardized by something as easy as maintaining a restroom! Furthermore, it makes me think more broadly that they are running a tight ship. That the kitchen is likely being maintained and cleaned appropriately. That the Department of Health inspections reveal nothing noteworthy. That I am eating in a clean restaurant. If a problem can be solved easily, act and fix it.

CASE STUDY

Let's talk Beavers!

What do you get when you combine a multi-category world record holder, unlikely pleasure destination, lauded barbeque sandwiches and beef jerky, one hundred gas pumps and award-winning clean restrooms...why, Buc-ee's of course! And I *am* a Beaver Believer. Some quick stats and quotes regarding the most famous beaver in the United States:

- It holds the world record for the World's Largest Convenience Store at 75,593 square feet in Luling, Texas
- It advertises its pristine bathrooms for hundreds of miles along interstates and delivers, too—Buc-ee's bathrooms have won awards for their otherworldly cleanliness
- "Buc-ee's has remained committed to providing award-winning clean restrooms, freshly prepared food, cheap gas, and outstanding customer service." *Jeff Nadalo, General Counsel, Buc-ee's*
- "People are so used to being let down when they stop at a restroom. It's so simple. It's a nice, well-lit, clean facility." *Founder Arch "Beaver" Aplin*
- "It's a fact that the cleaner the bathrooms, the more people will stop." *Nicholas Pell, CEO of Gas Station Management*

- "Bathrooms are the 'most important' component of the convenience store experience to nail if a business wants repeat customers. If they're pristine, like Buc-ee's claims its bathrooms are, then that impressed patron's curiosity is piqued, and they might spend more time perusing. You start there, at the restroom. Your perception of the store is tied to what the bathroom looks like. If it's good, you're going to shop. If it's not, you're going to leave. Stellar bathrooms can sell an awful lot of products." *Jeff Lenard, Vice President of Strategic Industry Initiatives at the National Association of Convenience Stores*
- Dylan and Shelby Reese, a husband-and-wife TikTok team, have been loyal Buc-ee's customers since the chain first arrived in Alabama in 2019. In June 2023, they created a video of their visit that's been viewed more than 6.7 million times! Million!

Buc-ee's leadership has clearly figured in to their business model the value that a clean restroom can provide. They know the time, energy and costs behind keeping them pristine are being returned many times over.

So, I ask again, do you place enough emphasis on restroom cleanliness and replenishment?

PART III

FINAL THOUGHTS

Conclusion

IT'S GO TIME!

Now, it is time to act on those items that you have realized could use some attention.

In today's post-pandemic environment, why do you think some restaurants clearly excel over others?

> *"Execution of the small details..."* Make sure to do these well because they add up. The larger details are easily noticed. But the smaller ones are more easily missed and can make or break an otherwise perfect dining experience.

STEPHEN SIDLO
Anthony's Coal Fired Pizza

"Because they took the opportunity during the pandemic to pivot and to reinvent themselves to the next level. They examined their existing methods and developed ways to improve upon them and create an even better guest experience. They embraced challenges and tested new ways of doing business in the post pandemic environment."

ELENA HERSHEY
Billy's Stone Crab

"Consistency in (quality) standards…" Whatever you do, do it to the best of your ability. All of my staff perform to the best of their ability. The hosts, bussers, servers, managers, and cashiers are all friendly and have positive attitudes. I like to call it 'Infectious positivity.'"

GARVIN MOISE
First Watch

A FEW THINGS TO REMEMBER WHILE TAKING YOUR JOURNEY…

- The host charging ahead when walking the guest to the table (negative); knowing which person at a full four-top receives which beverage without asking (positive); placing a dish by crossing an arm *in front of* the guest (negative); placing each meal without guidance, *"position point is paramount"* (positive); no paper towels in the restrooms (negative); *not* grabbing the beverage glass from the top (positive); having each meal brought to the table at the same time (positive); the guest receiving a departing remark from the host (positive)…

- Why do *you* go to a restaurant? What do *you* expect?

- Put out great content, quality photos. People look and save the places that catch their eyes. You need great content in today's world

- New hire evaluation periods

- "The whole is greater than the sum of its parts"—Aristotle

- "Don't sweat the small stuff"— "Focus on the big picture"— "*See* the forest but be mindful of the trees"

- In today's environment, unless you're focused on a specific segment and have "niched down," a successful restaurant needs to get *all of it right*

- It is the culmination of *many things*

- "Soft skills enhance customer service: Jobs that involve interacting with customers, clients, or patients require strong soft skills like communication, problem-solving, and empathy. It's the soft skills that enable employees to provide excellent customer service"—Greg Goldshteyn

- If something appeared sub-standard, would the server, your first line of defense, know how to react and act if necessary?

- "Don't be a champion of the mediocre"—Judith R. Faulkner

- "Be willing to make decisions. That's the most important quality in a good leader. Don't fall victim to what I call the Ready, Aim-Aim-Aim Syndrome. You must be willing to fire"—T. Boone Pickens

- How many restaurants are within three miles of yours and *why* would someone choose yours?

- Remember your decided goals and "failing fast"

- Retaining a customer is much cheaper than acquiring a new one

- "Online presence isn't just important; it is *majorly important.* In today's world, if you're not communicating with your guests online, you're invisible"—*Elena Hershey*

- Loyalty programs can help your restaurant retain customers

- If a problem can be solved easily, act and fix it

- "You never get a second chance to make a first impression"

- They've decided to go out to eat at *your* restaurant and they ended up in *your* section

- Just like the dishwasher, the expediter and food runner play important roles

- It truly *is* a team effort

- Consider providing something of perceived value in exchange for survey responses

- Let's talk Beavers!

- Keep in mind which works best for *your* restaurant

Appendix

RESTAURANT
GLOSSARY

The restaurant business has a language all its own, with the most common terms being used across most restaurant types. This makes communication among staff members more efficient. By no means is this list exhaustive, and undoubtedly, unfamiliar terms will be acquired on the job. The definitions and specific duties outlined should be modified to best suit the restaurant's needs.

JARGON—TERM	DEFINITION
A La Carte	A food item served by itself, typically on its own dish, and charged separately (whereas side dishes typically *accompany* the main dish and are included in the main dish price).

All Day	An expression used by a chef to indicate the total number of items to be prepared by the kitchen at the same time—e.g., two separate tickets arrive, and each have a Lobster Thermidor and sautéed Brussels sprouts. The chef may yell out "two Lobster Thermidor, two Brussel sprouts all day," meaning he needs two dishes of each to be prepared at that time.
Appetizer (App)	Typically, a small dish intended to be consumed before the main dish and often accompanied by a beverage.
AUV	Average unit volume: Franchise AUV stands for average unit volume, which is the average sales for each location. It represents the average annual sales volume of individual franchise units within a franchise system. This figure is calculated by dividing the total sales of all units by the number of units.
Back of House (BOH)	The area of a restaurant where guests are not allowed—e.g., kitchen, dishwashing, food prep areas.
Bakery Chef	See Pastry Chef.
Barback	Assists the bartender by managing a number of duties. For example: restocking glasses, flatware, table settings, liquor, beer, ice, condiments, napkins, straws; wiping down surfaces; removing trash; making coffee. The dishwasher may also perform these duties.
Bar Manager	For bars within restaurants, they manage the staff (possibly hiring), shift scheduling, inventory and collaborate with the general manager.

"Behind" (you, said aloud)	When approaching a co-worker that cannot see you, say aloud "Behind" or "Behind You" to alert them. This is especially important if their hands are full of plates or drinks. This term (and "hot") is also used in the kitchen.
BOH Manager	Manages the BOH staff and operations including the kitchen, dry and cold storage, dishwashing. Supply ordering, inventory, health regulations, staff hiring, training and scheduling could fall under their watch.
Bullet (cup, ramekin)	A small cup to hold a small portion of, typically, sauce.
Bus (bussing), Busser	To bus a table is to clear the table of the prior diners' dishes, glasses and utensils and reset with clean ones. Along with the servers, bussers should ensure the table condiments have adequate content and are clean. In addition, bussers may oversee small chores such as providing guests with additional table setting items and refilling non-alcoholic beverages. They may assist other staff members in their duties, including restocking items and seating guests.
Bussing Station	Instead of having to take dirty table items directly to the dishwashing area, bus stations are situated in the FOH with the purpose of creating a more efficient way to quickly clear a table. Typically, these stations will have trash receptacles, storage, stocked sealed table condiments and multiple dish tubs for easy transport to the dishwashing, all to improve service efficiency. Note, the station should be strategically located to avoid a negative guest experience by way of excessive noise or foot traffic.

Camper	A guest that remains at the table for an extended period, usually longer than one would normally. This can apply either before or after the check has been dropped.
Carry	This refers to the actual carrying of the food or drinks. Co-workers may comment "nice carry," indicating they approve and that the person is carrying numerous plates or drinks simultaneously.
Chaffing Dish	A metal dish filled with water and a heating source underneath. Frequently used on buffets.
Check Presenter/Guest Check Holder	The check could be presented (dropped) in a number of ways from the traditional black faux leather or plastic bi-fold container to a mini wooden clipboard. The check should be presented in a way that is commensurate with the restaurant/dining experience.
Chef (aka Kitchen Manager)	Chefs are trained cooks that have an elevated level of responsibility in, and for, the kitchen. The Head Chef typically cooks and manages the staff, budget, menus, specials, recipes, major cleaning schedules around best practices and departments of health. Hierarchically, the Head Chef (aka Kitchen Manager) would be below the Executive Chef and BOH Manager.
Comped	Comped, or complimentary, is something provided for free—typically when the guest has had a bad UX caused by underperforming staff or poor food quality.

"Corner" (BOH), said aloud	When restaurant employees approach a blind corner in the kitchen they yell out "Corner" to notify others of their presence and to remove the possibility of a collision. This is important when food is being carried out from around the blind corner. Let them know you are there!
Cowboy/Texas Caviar	Recipes vary but most combine a Pico de Gallo-type base mixed with corn, black-eyed peas, black beans, corn, bell peppers, avocados and a vinaigrette-style dressing.
Cut (being)	When a server is cut, they are no longer assigned new tables: they finish serving existing guests and begin their sidework. Conversely, a "stay" would be the server that closes the restaurant.
Dishwasher	Cleans all FOH tableware items—e.g., dishes, glasses, flatware and BOH kitchen equipment such as pots, pans, ladles, baking sheets. Restocks the line and expeditor areas of tableware items. General kitchen cleaning and assisting duties and possibly some FOH duties.
Double Sat, Triple Sat...	A server simultaneously sat at multiple tables, hence double (two tables), triple (three tables).
Double Shift aka back-to-back	Restaurants typically have day or night shifts. The hours will vary depending on the position—e.g., 7 AM to 3 PM, 3 PM to 11 PM. If an employee works two consecutive shifts, they will have worked a "double shift" or "back-to-back" shifts.
Dry Storage	Items not requiring refrigeration. It can contain food and non-food items—e.g., pots, pans, linens, canned goods, spices, coffee, flour and pasta.

Eighty-Five (85)	Some restaurants will "85" an item to indicate one is remaining. This puts the servers on notice that the item may not be available, and they can forewarn their customers.
Eighty-Six (86)	If the kitchen can no longer prepare a particular dish because an ingredient is missing or it cannot be prepared up to their standards, they will inform the staff it is "86," meaning that it is no longer available for purchase. The term's origin is unknown. Explanations from Wikipedia: Part of the jargon used by soda jerks e.g., 81 was a glass of water and 86 meant "all out of it." Author Jef Klein theorized that the bar Chumley's at 86 Bedford Street in the West Village of Lower Manhattan was the source. He claims that the police would call Chumley's bar during Prohibition before making a raid and tell the bartender to "86" his customers, meaning that they should exit out the 86 Bedford Street door.
Entrée	In the United States, the entrée typically refers to the main dish. In other countries, it could mean hors d'oeuvre or appetizer.
Executive Chef	Most Executive Chefs no longer cook but take on more managerial duties and are responsible for the overall operation of the kitchen. As the senior kitchen staff role, they take on several duties that could include overall kitchen operations, leading the culinary team, ordering supplies, creating recipes, developing menus, cost and inventory control.

Expeditor	A kitchen staff member who confirms the ticket and then groups plated food together by table number to prepare it for table delivery. They may also add condiments and garnishments. They stand on the server side of the line in a designated expeditor area.
Fast Casual	Offers the convenience and speed of a fast-food restaurant but without table service. Generally, they will offer a nicer ambiance and higher-quality food.
Fine Dining	Higher-quality food, service and ambiance will characterize these eateries.
Fire (BOH)	To start cooking or preparing a dish immediately. The cook may yell out "fire the main courses for table X!" or "chocolate soufflés for private party, fire!"
Front of House (FOH)	The area of a restaurant where guests are allowed—e.g., dining room, bar, foyer, restrooms.
FOH Manager	The FOH manager will oversee all front of house team members—e.g., servers, hosts, sommeliers. Responsibilities may include defining the hiring processes of all new FOH job applicants; shift scheduling; conflict resolution; training; POS daily closings; next shift/day readiness and other administrative duties. They will also work with other managers. They need to ensure a positive UX for the guests by monitoring staff, running interference when needed and proactively interacting with guests to ensure their experience is a positive one.

Follow	Typically, this is a new server—e.g., a new server that is in training would be the "follow" of the experienced server.
Food Aggregators	Food aggregators, or food delivery aggregators, are third-party companies that offer a single online platform for handling restaurant meal ordering, delivery and customer service. Think Uber Eats, DoorDash, Grubhub.
General Manager (GM)	The GM manages the entire operation—i.e., the BOH and FOH—and is the glue, or connection, between the two areas. As the go-to person, they are to ensure smooth operation as they have visibility into all aspects of the business. They should interact frequently with guests to validate the restaurant's goals are being met.
High-Top Table	A high-top is characterized by a table height taller (40–42 inches) than a traditional table height (29–30 inches). These afford the guests an elevated position over traditional tables and booth heights. Typically, these are in the bar area of a restaurant.
Host/Hostess/Greeter	(At the host stand/counter:) The person who greets the guests and shows them to their tables, but they typically have additional responsibilities too. The primary focus is the organized process of seating guests across the restaurant's sections to ensure all servers receive an equitable share of diners. If possible, this would include larger parties—e.g., 8–12 guests.
In The Biz	In the restaurant industry, "in the biz" means working within the broader hospitality sector, specifically in establishments that serve food and drinks, such as restaurants, bars and cafes.

In The Weeds	This term refers to the kitchen or a position (e.g., server) that is terribly busy. When the kitchen is in the weeds, it means they are running behind with fulfilling orders. If a server or bartender is in the weeds, they are personally very busy and running behind and potentially providing a less-than-ideal guest user experience. For example, if the kitchen has numerous order tickets and is having a challenging time keeping up, they are "in the weeds."
KDS	Kitchen Display System—replaces handwritten or paper ticket orders.
Kitchen Manager	See Chef.
Line (the)	The line is the area that divides the cooks from the wait staff and expeditor. It is where the food is prepared and placed to await pickup. Multiple lines can exist that specialize in preparation of a particular food type or style.
Line Cook	A line cook (aka commis, section, station chef, chef de partie) typically works on a dedicated section of the line and on an assigned shift. They are proficient in their line area type (e.g., grill, sauté) or food type (e.g., fish, meats) and can receive orders from higher-level chefs.
LTO	Limited-Time Offer is a menu item, or multiple items, only available for a limited time.
Main Course (dish)	Typically, the primary course, with side dishes built around it. Commonly, the main ingredient is a protein such as fish or meat, and this dish would follow an appetizer and be followed by a dessert.

Maître d' aka maître d'hôtel	Maître d' (French phrase for "master of" and short for maître d'hôtel) is typically the head of the dining room staff.
Mise En Place	A French phrase that means "set up," "putting in place," "gathering," "everything in its place." For efficiency, cooks put their cookware and ingredients in a certain spot for their shift—e.g., salt and pepper to the right, oils to the left, 10" sauté pans directly above on a shelf. Everything is prepared and put in its place prior to cooking.
On Deck (BOH)	This term is to communicate to the dish's server, food runner or kitchen that an order is coming up soon and not to leave the area if you're the server or food runner, or to be aware if you're the line cook of what's coming up and to be prepared.
On The Fly (BOH)	When something unexpected must be cooked urgently, for example, when an order mistake has occurred or additional items are needed.
On The Side (OTS)	When an item is asked to be on the side of the main dish—e.g., salad dressings are frequently asked to be "on the side."
Open Hand(s); "Hands" (BOH)	This is a literal description of one's hand(s) being available or "open" to carry a plate of food or drink to a table. This person is usually "running food or drink" for another server and not their own. The cooks may state "hands" to request assistance in delivering a large order to a table or a fellow server may ask for "open hands" to assist in bringing food or drinks to their table.

Pastry Chef	aka dessert chef or pâtissier: a chef that specializes in and prepares items such as desserts, cakes, cookies and pastries. They will create new recipes and be responsible for managing all necessary facets to do their job, such as stocking the necessary ingredients, staff guidance and working cookware.
Pick Up (kitchen)	To indicate a dish is ready to be taken to the guest—e.g., Pickup table X or Y would tell the server that their table's food was ready.
Pick Up Shift	To "pick up a shift" is to work a shift that was not previously scheduled—e.g., can you pick up a Friday night shift (where you were not already on the schedule).
Pick Up Table	To "pick up a table" is to add another table to a section that was not previously assigned—e.g., can you pick up table 50 (where that table is normally assigned to another section).
Plate/Plating (food)	This is the act of placing and arranging the food on a plate (plated). This includes adding any sauce or garnish before handing over to the expeditor or the server.
POS (point of sale)	A point of sale system is a computer system that can assist a business in tracking sales, inventory levels, specific dish sales and myriad other items.

Pour Cost (individual drink)	Individual drink costs are determined by first calculating the cost of the drink's liquor content in ounces, by dividing the *bottle's* cost by the number of ounces per bottle. Then calculate the individual costs of all other drink items—e.g., mixers, garnishments, juices, fruit wedges. Sum the liquor and the other ingredient costs. Divide this cost by the price of the drink to arrive at the pour cost percentage.
Prep Cook	This position is a member of the kitchen responsible for readying the ingredients that will be used by the line cooks when making the dishes. This could include creating meat and fish portions; preparing sauces, salad mixes, juices and dressings; cutting vegetables and storing them appropriately in the kitchen or on the line.
QSR	"Quick Service Restaurant," typically without table service, aka Fast-Food Restaurant.
Reach-In (Refrigerator)	Commercial refrigerator with a solid or glass door where the user "reaches in" for anything needing refrigeration and quick access—i.e., items consumed on a consistent basis.
Reggae	If an item is ordered "Reggae" it indicates to the kitchen that the item is "without modification" or "regular" and should be prepared as presented or stated in the menu.
Running (items)	The transport of food, drinks, utensils, condiments or other needed items to a table: "Run X to table 18." Most FOH personnel can run items, but food and drinks are typically reserved for Servers or Food Runners.

Salamander Kitchen	A piece of kitchen equipment with a large heating element on the top (producing a higher temperature than standard broilers) designed for e.g., browning, grilling, broiling, melting cheese, caramelizing, finishing.
Section/Station	Typically, a restaurant dining room is divided into multiple sections that each have a server(s) assigned for each shift. A station can have an identification name or number with four to five tables, each of which have their own number or name. Section numbering needs to be logical to be easily understood by staff. As closing time approaches, the number of sections is usually reduced, with wait staff being cut for the night and the remaining servers closing out the evening. They are known as "closers" or "stays" and are "closing."
Server/Waitstaff	aka waitress/waiter—the person assigned to a table and its guests to take their orders, provide service during their stay, confirm and ensure the guests are having a wonderful experience and provide the check/bill at the end of the occasion.
Setting	A table setting is the arrangement of the items placed on the table—e.g., plates, flatware, glasses, napkins, condiments. A "rollup" or "silverware roll" or "silverware bundle" is a napkin rolled up around utensils.
Shark Food	A term we used at TGI Fridays for dishes that were returned uneaten or deemed not acceptable by the BOH to be brought to the table. This food was placed in a location where the restaurant staff could eat it for free…hence, we called it "shark food."

Sidework (FOH, BOH)	Sidework (or side work) is a frequent practice in restaurants, occurring in both the front and back of house. These "housekeeping tasks" are performed daily to keep the business running smoothly and to improve the guests' experience. Sidework allows the restaurant to operate more smoothly and help provide the best guest experience. All refillable/consumable items should be verified adequately filled/available. Performing sidework is common after certain team members have been cut from their shift. BOH examples: Wash all dirty dishes, glasses, utensils, pots, pans, sheets; restock all dishes, pots, pans, cooking utensils on the line; restock the expeditor area's to-go containers, condiments, utensil settings; all dry garnishments on the line and expeditor area. FOH examples: Refill/replace all condiments, fold napkins, wipe down the entire table, organize tabletop items, replace old/broken tabletop items, create napkin rollups with utensils.
Signature Dish	These dishes are unique creations identified by, and exclusive to, a particular chef or restaurant while representing their style and expertise. A signature dish applies evolved experience and reflects the style of its creator while incorporating local or regional influences and helping to create a restaurant's identity.

Slammed	A slammed restaurant or section is simply terribly busy. This could be temporary, for example, if a server had three tables all sat at the same time. Or the restaurant could be remarkably busy the entire night with a constant wait for new tables.
Smallware	The term "smallware" encompasses hundreds of various products—everything from utensils to cookware for the kitchen, and glassware to dinnerware for the dining room. Cleaning supplies including mops, brooms and buckets are also considered smallware. Smallware includes all glassware, flatware, dinnerware, pots and pans, tabletop items, bar supplies, food preparation utensils and tools, storage supplies, service items and small appliances costing $500 or less.
SOS	Term used by servers when entering an order in the POS, or writing it on a paper ticket, to indicate to the kitchen that the sauce is SOS "sauce on side"—i.e., it should be put on the side.
Sous Chef	"Sous" from the French meaning "under" is a chef that works directly under the executive chef or chef de cuisine. In other words, the second in command.
A Stay	For multi-shift operations, the "Stay" would be the person that would stay until the restaurant closes (the last shift).
Table Sharing (Community Table)	A shared large table to accommodate a group of unrelated diners. Benefits include increased space utilization, meals served, reduced guest wait times and friendly interactions.

Ticket (kitchen)	A written, or POS-generated, list of menu items ordered by the guest for the kitchen to prepare, including: the server's name, item quantities, special requests, table number, time entered (into POS).
Turn Restaurant	Turning a restaurant is the number of times each table has been sat with a unique party. This is a cumulative number referring to all tables in the restaurant. For example, a restaurant with 40 tables saying "we turned the restaurant two times last night" would mean that each table was seated two times during the evening for a total of 80 tables having had different dinner guests.
Turn Table	Turning a table is the number of times a particular table has been sat, cleared and reset with new table settings. If a particular table had three unique parties during a shift it could be said the table was "turned" three times in this time.
Two Top, Four Top…	Term to describe how many guests would customarily sit at a table—e.g., two people, four persons.
Unique Selling Point or Proposition (USP)	A restaurant's focus on how to achieve a product- or service-based unique selling point or proposition (USP) with the goal of differentiating itself from other eating establishments. This could include a unique location or inside built-out feature, food items, drink items, decor…
User, or Guest, Experience (UX)	Providing the best experience for the guest when they enter the business's environment and interact with its team members.

Walk-In Refrigerator	Insulated refrigerated or freezer room accessible via a door where product is stored, typically used for larger goods and items not consumed rapidly; extra/inventoried goods.
Waxing a Table (FOH)	An expression to tell a server to treat a specific table like a VIP.
"Window" aka the Pass	The "window" is the area in front of the line where chefs place the prepared dishes for server pickup. If staffed, the expeditor would stand here.

ABOUT THE AUTHOR

Deryk D. Davidson has developed a practical understanding of restaurant operations through hands-on experience in both kitchen and service environments, including line cooking at Boulder's iconic Nancy's Restaurant and guest-experience roles at high-volume establishments such as Aventura's TGI Fridays, the second-busiest location in South Florida.

His perspective is further shaped by years of observing and engaging with restaurant teams across 42 states, allowing him to identify recurring challenges, effective practices, and the differentiators that set successful restaurants apart—from casual cafés to fine dining venues.

For those interested in continued dialogue through consulting or speaking, contact the author at HospitalityEdge.net.